C#

Simple and Effective Tips and Tricks to Learn C# Programming Effectively

BENJAMIN SMITH

Table of Contents

Introduction

This book contains proven steps and strategies on how to program in C# or C Sharp. This book will help you learn the basics of C# programming simply and effectively. I have written and tested all the code samples that I have included in the book. You have the permission to copy the code and paste in the editor or compiler to see the results. I recommend that in the first attempt you should copy and paste the code to have a feel of how you a program in C# looks like. When you think that you have acquired sufficient knowledge and have also refurbished your programming skills, you can edit the sample codes by changing variable names, class names, values of the integers, and add more class instances. Afterward, you can compile the code and see the results.

You should not worry if you don't see the desired results and see an error message instead. I have dedicated a comprehensive section on what possible errors you may come across during the programming phase and what the error message will look like. All you need is to study the error message and understand its context. Then you can easily remove the errors and streamline the code. When you have gained expertise in reading and understanding the error messages, you will make fewer errors.

C# programming language is a powerful language. It is relatively mature and is a descendant of C and C++. It also retains certain features of the Java language. Programming with C# is great fun. Microsoft created C# as a part of the .NET initiative. This book will explain the ins and outs of C# programming language. You will learn how to write usable programs. For which purpose, you will need a particular coding environment. We bet that most of the readers will definitely use Microsoft Visual Studio. There are alternatives that you can lay your hands on.

I learned to program when I was in high school. I didn't study programming in the school or college. Instead, I learned it by reading a bunch of good books and practice. My love for coding started with an incident. I used to study history at school. Like all the other teenagers, I was in love with my computer and the internet. One day I was coming back from school to home. It was a dull afternoon. The sky had gone behind thick clouds when I put my car on the highway. It was a beautiful sight and scary too. The line of trees along the edge of the road had starts swaying back and forth being pushed by gusts of wind. I knew a storm was likely to hit the town. And it did. It went dark suddenly. I was afraid, to say the least. It rained heavily that afternoon. The wind smashed the car windows but I kept driving until I got out of the storm. I reached home by evening only to find that my system applications had been shattered in a hacking attack. I used to run an online application that I had got developed by a friend. I wondered if he would develop the same from scratch again. He refused to cite the reason that he had been busy in research work. I was disappointed, to say the least. He ruined my life.

That day I decided to take over the control of developing my applications. I learned C# along with other programming languages and I found it the best out of all of them. My craze for coding didn't stop there but it increased several folds. I built one after another application and also sold some to fellow students.

What This Book Has for You

This book is the best for those who want to learn C# programming from scratch. Every beginner should read this book. You don't have to be an expert programmer to benefit from the knowledge in this book. This book is divided into chapters that deal with different topics. The book contains code samples for each feature of C# I explain. To make the samples easier to understand, I must say that I have written them in an editor. The editor usually has two parts; one part pertains to the written code space where you write. The other part pertains to space where you can see the compiled results. I have shown the two spaces with a single line between the two so that you may understand the program in a better way. This is how you can match your results with mine. If there is a difference, you can double-check the written code and match it with mine to see where you have missed. Sometimes, programmers misspell a word at two different spots. At other times, programmers fail to keep up the cases of the words in check. They use uppercase for the first letter at one point and use lowercase for the same letter at another point. This can make practicing a frustrating job. However, if you do it carefully and wisely, you can keep these errors in check.

The first chapter will explain to you what C# is. You will learn about the working of a visual studio. Visual studio is a compiler in which you can write your code and compile a program. I will explain in this section how you can download visual studio and install it on your system. You will also learn how you can use it to write and compile C# programs. The next section of the book is about creating the console program. The chapter ends with saving the code.

The second chapter of the book deals with getting started with C# programming. You will learn about writing C# strings. If you are acquainted with programming languages, you might know what strings are and how you can use them while writing a program. A string is a data type that can store a piece of text. You can fill it in a thousand pages of text if your program demands it. The text which is stored in a string is generally stored as a collection of Char objects. String objects are immutable and you cannot change them after you have created them. All the string methods and operators that seem like modifying a string tend to return the results as a new string object. You can create as many strings for your program as you need. It will not overfill the program. After defining the string, the chapter will move on to explaining the comparison of strings. The next section of the chapter will shed light on the length of strings and string methods as well. You can concatenate strings which, in simple language, means that you can add together two strings. You will have to use a new variable to transfer the results of the addition of the strings.

The chapter further moves on to explain C# arrays and lists. You will learn how you can create an array in C#. I will explain with an easy-t0-digest example. You will get the opportunity to create an array by adding different objects to the array. You can create an array first and then keep adding different objects to the same along the way. The next section of the chapter will explain how you can know what the length of an array is. The chapter then glides down to explain how you loop through an array. Once you have created an array, you can remove its items by a simple method. I will explain how to do that. This can be useful if you are creating a game in which a character sells fruits.

When the fruit is sold out, the player can have the opportunity to remove them one by one. The last section of this chapter explains lists. I will start by getting you acquainted with different methods of creation of lists. You can create a list that contains numbers and you also can create a list that contains pieces of texts such as names of vegetables and fruits. Once you have familiarized yourself with how you create lists, you can move on to learning how to remove items from a list. There are two methods to do that. One method relates to directly removing items by using names. The other method is by removing items by using the index number. Fill in the list methods with an index number and afterward let C# count the remaining items. You will get the total number minus the removed item. There is a dedicated method for concatenation in C#

programming language which I will explain at the end of the chapter.

The third chapter of the book revolves around conditionals. Conditional statements are the keys to testing certain conditions, perform mathematical functions, and display interactive messages to users when they use your program. The first in the line is the if statement. I will explain by code samples how you can create an if statement and for which purpose you can use them while building a program. The next section of the chapter deals with the else statement which is a step further to the if statement. If one statement stands false, the else statement is put to work. It takes the rest of the code to a conclusion. The third section deals with the else-if statement. It forms the third block of code in the construction of the conditionals. Now there are three conditions at work. I will explain how you can use three conditionals to test different conditions and build complex programs. The chapter ends on explaining the shorthand else-if statement. These statements are recommended only for seasoned programmers who can easily understand written code even if it is written on the same line. Otherwise, the lengthy method is the best to choose and try.

The fourth chapter of the book is about interactive programming using C#. The first section of the book focuses on user input. You can invite the users to fill your program with the type of information that you need from them. The second section specifies the type of input that you want your users to add to the program.

The third section of the book focuses on the switch statement and the usage of the break keyword.

The fifth section of the book deals with C# loops. You will learn what a while loop is and how you can create it in C#. The while loop in C# programming language is the same as in any other programming language. You can write it and use it to create a program that repeats and tests the condition as long as it stands true. It stops at the point the condition stands false. The next on the line is nested while loop. You can nest it inside of the main while loop to create a combination in which one while loop will test each navigation of the first loop. I have written a sample code that you can paste in the compiler you are using and test what happens. The next section of the chapter focuses on the do-while loop and a nested do-while loop. In this chapter, you will learn what for loops are, how you can create them, and what purpose they are written for. You will get to learn multiple expressions regarding the for a loop. You will also learn about what nested for loops are. I will explain the significance of foreach loop to sort out arrays. The chapter has something really interesting in common. If you know how to drive, you know how to put the brakes on and push the paddle. Of course, you will have code samples to practice the break and continue statements so that you can learn in a better way.

The sixth chapter of the book deals with methods. If you are aware of Python, you may know that Python has functions that you can create and call later on. The best thing about Python functions is that you can create them once and use them as many times as you need. They cut down the coding time, and also save you from the hassle of writing the same code again and again for different purposes. This is why functions are considered the lifeline of Python. As Python has functions to offer, C# has methods. They do just the same thing that functions do. You can create them once and use them at will. The first section of this chapter defines what methods are. The second section of the chapter explains what parameters are, how you can create them, and how you can pass them to the methods to create a program. You also can use multiple parameters to pass on to C# methods. In the next section of this chapter, I will explain how you can return values in a method. You can do calculations and store the result in a separate variable. This is how methods work.

The seventh chapter of the book deals with object-oriented programming. The first section of the chapter helps you create a C# class, the same as classes in Python or Java. They serve the purpose of creating real-life models or objects. For example, I will create a Cat class or a Dog class. I will then give them certain attributes that real cats and dogs possess. After educating on how to create a C# class, I will explain how you can create a car class. This program can help you if you run a car showroom. You can add instances in the car class whenever you receive a new car for the showroom. The instance will act as a new object and will be stored in the database of the program. This is how you can build a powerful program that can serve your commercial needs. I will shed light on class members and class methods. The class constructor is one of the most interesting topics in the book. It makes making classes easier for you. It guides you and cuts down the steps for making classes. You can pass multiple parameters to a class, but I will explain that by example. The chapter ends on explaining what C# properties are how you can use them for your benefit.

The eight-chapter of the book carries an in-depth explanation of C# classes. You will learn in this chapter a bunch of interesting concepts such as polymorphism, interfaces, and abstraction. All these concepts belong to C# classes. At the end of the chapter, I will try to educate you on different error messages. C# is a compiled language. Python developers can see through the error easily as the editor or terminal mentions the line on which you have made the error. However, C# doesn't offer such a privilege. Therefore, I have explained different types of error messages as to how they look and what are the driving factors behind each error message. You can feed the messages in mind to familiarize yourself with them so that you may be able to detect them and fix them when you hit one

The ninth chapter is the last of the book. In this chapter, I will explain how to write secure code and what types of attacks you may experience in your programs. The first topic of this chapter is about building a secure design for your program. The next topic is about the documentation of the threat like defining its nature, defining the scope of the attack, and analyzing the extent of the damage the attack can inflict on your application. At the end of the chapter, I will give you a brief glimpse of STRIDE which explains different types of attacks on applications.

In conclusion, I will explain how C# can benefit you and why you should immediately switch to C# programming. You will have more than one reason to do that if you read it carefully.

Everyone who has the basic knowhow of programming can read this book. Even if you are a novice in the world of programming, this book will walk you through the world of C# and help you learn the basics. You can practice and reach the advanced programming level gradually. I recommend that you grab a notebook, a pen, and a laptop when you start reading the book. It is a technical book and you should read it like that. Once you read a brief for a C# feature and go through the sample code, you should write it down or use it in a compiler for practice. The more you practice each sample code by using it as it is and by editing the same by making small changes to have a feeling that you are writing the code yourself. Make sure you keep track of the changes or you will not be able to fix any errors that may pop up.

The book is an interesting read and by the time you have made it to the end, you will be equipped with the basics and the advanced levels of C# programming. You will be able to write real programs that are based on Object-Oriented Programming (OOP) which is the most popular aspect of C# language.

Chapter One

What Is C#?

The C# programming language is one of the languages that programmers use to build executable programs. C# is a powerful object-oriented language. It is open-source, modern, simple, and flexible, and is also quite a versatile language. A programming language is something that you can use to write software programs. C# is a simple language that also supports modern-day functionality for different types of software development. C# was designed in the first place to help enterprises and businesses. It caters to all of their needs. It was designed to build different software for businesses. C# provides much-needed functionality to support modern-day software development. It supports mobile and web app development.

C# is open source under .NET Foundation. Microsoft governs and runs the foundation. C# language compilers, specifications, and tools can be found as open-source projects on GitHub.

C# is flexible as the programs built with it can be executed on the current machine or they can simply be transmitted on the Web. You also can execute them on some distant computer. C# is powerful because it has the same command set as that of C++. It error-proofs the commands that are responsible for several C++ errors so that you spend less time chasing them down.

The .NET code library that C# uses for its capabilities offers the help that is needed to create complicated display frames, including drop-down lists, grouped buttons, background images, tabbed windows, and scroll bars. C# tends to play a pivotal role in the .NET Framework.

What Is Visual Studio?

Programmers label Visual Studio an Integrated Development Environment (IDE). This IDE aids you in creating native code and managed code as well. Visual Studio was released in 1997 and since then it has been considerably evolved. The latest version is known as Visual Studio 2017. The details of the three versions of Microsoft Visual Studio are as follows.

Community

This is a free version. The features are much more the same as of the professional editions. You can use this edition to develop an application such as web applications and .NET applications. However, if you want it for an enterprise organization, you may have to face some limitations. If your organization has revenue above $1 million a year, you cannot use this free version. You can code in JavaScript, C#, Python, F#, HTML and Python by using this free version.

Professional Version

This is the commercial edition that offers support for XSLT and XML editing. You also can integrate it with Microsoft SQL Server. You can download and install it for a free trial to get a knowhow of its unique and additional features. You will get professional tools for developing apps. Features like CodeLens tend to improve the productivity of your team.

Enterprise Version

This version is an end-t0-end solution for big teams that have unique quality demands. You can get a 90-day free trial for this version. When the trial period ends, you can pay for it to continue using it. One of the major benefits of this edition is that you can build high-quality software.

There is a code editor in each version where you will get to write the code. Paired up with that is an output window where you can see the results of the code, error messages and warnings issued by the compiler.

You can create or save a project using the File menu, while the Edit menu offers modification and refactoring of different code commands. You can use the Project menu for adding different dependencies to the project.

Creating the Console Application

Microsoft Visual Studio 2010 carries an Application Wizard that tends to build template programs. It also saves you a lot of dirty work that you would have to do if you started from scratch. Starter programs don't do anything useful. However, they do get you beyond the initial hurdle of starting the development phase. Some of the starter programs are sophisticated. A console application is the one that runs in a console on your Windows. You can refer to it as the command window or DOS prompt. If you hit Ctrl + R and after that type cmd, a window will pop up on the screen. It is the console where your application will run.

To start Visual Studio, you need to choose to navigate to Start then All Programs then Microsoft Visual Studio. You will have to create a console app at the start. Open Visual Studio 2010 and hit the New Project icon. In the new window, select Visual C. You will be required to create a project before you enter your C# program. A project is like a folder in which you need to throw your files that make your program. You will get hold of a set of configuration files to aid the compiler is doing its job. The default place to store your files is in the Documents directory.

The default place to store the file is in the Documents directory. You also can change the default program location. Go to Choose Tools and click Options. You will see Choose Projects and Solutions. Click on the General and select the new location. Click Ok.

Saving Code

When you have written code, you can save it in a handy location to use in the future. That location is the Toolbox window. You have to follow these steps. In the Main() method of the class Program, you need to select the lines you have to save. Open the Toolbox window. Open it by choosing View and then click on Toolbox. Now drag the selected lines in the General tab onto the Toolbox window and drop the same. You can, anytime, reuse the code in the future.

Chapter Two

Getting Started With C#

The most basic concept is of variables in all programming languages. A C# variable, like that of other languages, is a small container that stores different things like numbers. The term variable comes from mathematics. In C# there are several limitations for programmers when it comes to using them to building programs. This chapter will walk you through the world of variables. You will learn how to declare them, initialize them, and use them in C#.

You might have learned in the third grade the equation $x = 1$. By writing the equation, you are declaring a variable. You are saying that the variable x has the value '1.' In the world of programming, you first have to define a variable in a specific way.

C# has different types of variables. The variable 'int' is used to store integers like whole numbers without decimals. The variable 'double' is used to store floating-point numbers such as 20.67. The variable 'char' is used to store single characters such as 'x'. You have to surround the char values within single quotes. The variable 'bool' is used to store values with two states such as false or true. The variable 'string' is used to store pieces of text; you will have to store string values by double-quotes.

If you want to create a variable, you must specify its type and its value as well. Assign the variable a name such as x and add an equal sign if you want to assign values to the variable. See the following variable that should store text.

```
using System.IO;
using System;
class myProgram
{
    static void Main(string[] args)
    {
        string sentence = "This is a C# program. I am creating a string by filling it in with a particular value!";
        Console.WriteLine(sentence);
    }
}
$mcs *.cs -out:main.exe
$mono main.exe
```

This is a C# program. I am creating a string by filling it in with a particular value!

In the following example, I will create a variable named thisNum in which I will store a number. Take a look at the following example. I will create a variable named thisNum of int type. Will also assign it a numeric value.

```
using System.IO;
using System;
class myProgram
{
    static void Main(string[] args)
    {
        int thisNum = 22;
        Console.WriteLine(thisNum);
    }
}
$mcs *.cs -out:main.exe
$mono main.exe
22
```

You also can create a variable first and assign the value later. See the following example.

```
using System.IO;
using System;
class myProgram
{
    static void Main(string[] args)
    {
        int thisNum;
        thisNum = 50;
        Console.WriteLine(thisNum);
```

```
        }
    }
$mcs *.cs -out:main.exe
$mono main.exe
50
```

If you have already assigned a value to a variable but you once again assign it in the next line, the previous value will be overwritten by the latest value.

```
using System.IO;
using System;
class myProgram
{
    static void Main(string[] args)
    {
        int thisNum = 25;
        thisNum = 50;
        Console.WriteLine(thisNum);
    }
}
$mcs *.cs -out:main.exe
$mono main.exe
50
```

C# Strings

A string is a class for which C# tends to offer special treatment because strings are widely used in several programs. The keyword string is often confused with String. In the following example, I will analyze different elements of a string.

```
using System.IO;
using System;
class myProgram
{
    static void Main(string[] args)
    {
        String sentence = "This is a C# program. I am creating a
string by filling it in with a particular value!";
        Console.WriteLine(sentence);
    }
}
```

In this example, a sentence is an object of the class String. If we convert the uppercase of S into lowercase, it will be a simple string. However, string or String is compatible with each other. Once you have created a string object, you cannot change or modify it. C# lacks an operation that tends to modify the string object. If you modify it, you will get a new object in return. That's how one string becomes two.

```
using System.IO;
using System;
namespace ModifyString
{
class Program
{
```

```
public static void Main(string[] args)
{
// I am now Create a brand student object.
newStudent s1 = new newStudent();
s1.Name = "Tom";
// Now I will make another new object that has the same
name.
newStudent s2 = new newStudent();
    s2.Name = s1.Name;
    s2.Name = s1.Name.ToUpper();
    Console.WriteLine("s1 - " + s1.Name + ", s2 - " +
    s2.Name);
    Console.WriteLine("You are required to Press the Enter
    button to terminate...");
    Console.Read();
    }
}
    class newStudent
    {
            public String Name;
            }
}
$mcs *.cs -out:main.exe
$mono main.exe
s1 - Tom, s2 - TOM
```

You are required to Press the Enter button to terminate...

The ToUpper didn't change the name. However, it created an independent uppercase string and the stores the same in the new object s2. This property of strings is also known as the immutability of unchangeability. It is important for string constants. As a C# programmer, you will get to perform multiple operations on strings. Every program tends to use an additional operator that you can use on strings. In the following example, I will use the + data operator to concatenate different pieces into one.

```
using System.IO;
using System;
namespace MyApplication
{
  class Program
  {
    static void Main(string[] args)
    {
      string name = "Tom";
      Console.WriteLine("I was pleased to meet him. His name
was " + name + ".");
    }

  }
}
$mcs *.cs -out:main.exe
$mono main.exe
```

I was pleased to meet him. His name was Tom.

Comparison of Strings

It is quite common to compare two strings. If you want to know whether two strings are equal in length or not, you can use the == operator to confirm. To see if they are unequal or not, you should use the inverse operator !=.

String Length

A string in C# language is an object, which contains methods and properties that would perform several operations on strings. For example, you can find the length of a string by using the Length property.

```
using System.IO;
using System;
namespace MyApplication
{
  class Program
  {
    static void Main(string[] args)
    {
      string sentence = "I am learning C Sharp. It is an
interesting object-oriented language.";
      Console.WriteLine("The length of the above mentioned
string is: " + sentence.Length);
    }


  }
}
```

```
$mcs *.cs -out:main.exe
$mono main.exe
```

The length of the above mentioned string is: 68

String Methods

There are different string methods that you can use. To name a few, you can convert strings into uppercase and lowercase by using some simple methods.

```
using System.IO;
using System;
namespace MyApplication
{
  class Program
  {
    static void Main(string[] args)
    {
      string sentence = "I am learning C Sharp. It is an
interesting object-oriented language.";
      Console.WriteLine(sentence.ToUpper());
    }

  }
}
$mcs *.cs -out:main.exe
$mono main.exe
```

I AM LEARNING C SHARP. IT IS AN INTERESTING OBJECT-ORIENTED LANGUAGE.

The above method converted the string to upper case. The following method will convert the string into the lower case. See the example.

```
using System.IO;
using System;
namespace MyApplication
{
  class Program
  {
    static void Main(string[] args)
    {
      string sentence = "I am learning C Sharp. It is an interesting object-oriented language.";
      Console.WriteLine(sentence.ToLower());
    }


  }
}
$mcs *.cs -out:main.exe
$mono main.exe
```

i am learning c sharp.it is an interesting object-oriented language.

There is a method to concatenate two strings. I will use the + operator to combine two strings into a single whole. See the following example for details.

```
using System.IO;
using System;
namespace MyApplication
{
  class Program
  {
    static void Main(string[] args)
    {
      string sentence1 = "I am learning C Sharp.";
      string sentence2 = "It is an interesting object-oriented language.";
      string fullsen = sentence1 + sentence2;
      Console.WriteLine(fullsen);
    }

  }
}
$mcs *.cs -out:main.exe
$mono main.exe
```

I am learning C Sharp. It is an interesting object-oriented language.

You can display the concatenated result in upper case as well by adding a simple method.

```
using System.IO;
using System;
namespace MyApplication
{
  class Program
  {
    static void Main(string[] args)
    {
      string sentence1 = "I am learning C Sharp.";
      string sentence2 = "It is an interesting object-oriented
language.";
      string fullsen = sentence1 + sentence2;
      Console.WriteLine(fullsen.ToUpper());
    }


  }
}
```
$mcs *.cs -out:main.exe
$mono main.exe

I AM LEARNING C SHARP. IT IS AN INTERESTING OBJECT-
ORIENTED LANGUAGE.

Now I will convert it into lowercase by adding the relevant method.

```
using System.IO;
using System;
namespace MyApplication
{
```

```
class Program
{
  static void Main(string[] args)
  {
    string sentence1 = "I am learning C Sharp.";
    string sentence2 = " It is an interesting object-oriented
language.";
    string fullsen = sentence1 + sentence2;
    Console.WriteLine(fullsen.ToLower());
  }


}
}
$mcs *.cs -out:main.exe
$mono main.exe
```

i am learning c sharp. it is an interesting object-oriented language.

String concatenation can also be done by using a dedicated concatenation method instead of the + operator. The method namely string.Concat() can be used to achieve the same goal.

```
using System.IO;
using System;
namespace MyApplication
{
  class Program
  {
    static void Main(string[] args)
```

```csharp
    {
        string sentence1 = "I am learning C Sharp.";
        string sentence2 = " It is an interesting object-oriented
language.";
        string fullsen = string.Concat (sentence1, sentence2);
        Console.WriteLine(fullsen.ToUpper());
    }


    }
}
$mcs *.cs -out:main.exe
$mono main.exe
```

I AM LEARNING C SHARP. IT IS AN INTERESTING OBJECT-ORIENTED LANGUAGE.

Another method for string concatenation is string interpolation, which substitutes the values of different variables into placeholders in the string. You should note that you don't have to worry about the spaces as is the case with concatenation.

```csharp
using System.IO;
using System;
namespace MyApplication
{
  class Program
  {
    static void Main(string[] args)
    {
```

```
    string sentence1 = "I am learning C Sharp.";
    string sentence2 = " It is an interesting object-oriented
language.";
    string fullsen = $"{sentence1} {sentence2}";
    Console.WriteLine(fullsen.ToUpper());
  }


 }
}
$mcs *.cs -out:main.exe
$mono main.exe
```

I AM LEARNING C SHARP.   IT IS AN INTERESTING
OBJECT-ORIENTED LANGUAGE.

Access String

There is a method to access different characters in a string by referring to the index number which is inside the square brackets.

```
using System.IO;
using System;
namespace MyApplication
{
  class Program
  {
    static void Main(string[] args)
    {
      string sentence1 = "I am learning C Sharp.";
```

```
    string sentence2 = " It is an interesting object-oriented
language.";
    Console.WriteLine(sentence1[9]);
  }


  }
}
$mcs *.cs -out:main.exe
Compilation succeeded - 1 warning(s)
main.cs(11,14): warning CS0219: The variable `sentence2' is
assigned but its value is never used
$mono main.exe
n
```

The compiler has issued a warning because I left the second string
without assigning any method to it. Let's access a character in the
second string.

```
using System.IO;
using System;
namespace MyApplication
{
  class Program
  {
    static void Main(string[] args)
    {
      string sentence1 = "I am learning C Sharp.";
```

```
    string sentence2 = " It is an interesting object-oriented
language.";
    Console.WriteLine(sentence1[10]);
    Console.WriteLine(sentence2[15]);
  }


  }
}
$mcs *.cs -out:main.exe
$mono main.exe
i
e
```

There is a reverse method by which you can locate the index number of each character in a string. All you have to do is to enter the alphabet of the string and C# will find the index number linked to that alphabet. There is a specific method for the purpose, called the IndexOf() method. I will use the same strings to test this method and see how effective it is when you are creating a program.

```
    using System.IO;
    using System;
    namespace MyApplication
    {
      class Program
      {
        static void Main(string[] args)
        {
```

```
    string sentence1 = "I am learning C Sharp.";
    string sentence2 = " It is an interesting object-oriented
language.";
        Console.WriteLine(sentence1.IndexOf("S"));
        Console.WriteLine(sentence2.IndexOf("t"));
    }


  }
}
$mcs *.cs -out:main.exe
$mono main.exe
16
2
```

Substrings

There is another useful method known as Substring() which extracts
several characters from a particular string. You can decide the
specified character position and the method will come up with a
new substring. I will use this method in combination with
IndexOf() to find out the specific character position.

```
using System.IO;
using System;
namespace MyApplication
{
  class Program
  {
    static void Main(string[] args)
```

```
        {
            string sentence2 = " It is an interesting object-oriented
language.";
          int charPos = sentence2.IndexOf("o");

          string sentence3 = sentence2.Substring(charPos);

          Console.WriteLine(sentence3);
            }

        }
    }
$mcs *.cs -out:main.exe
$mono main.exe
object-oriented language.
```

In the next example, I will choose another point from where I will slice off the substring. I will enter 'i' as the point from which the program should slice off the string and create a substring.

```
using System.IO;
using System;
namespace MyApplication
{
  class Program
  {
    static void Main(string[] args)
    {
```

```
    string sentence2 = " It is an interesting object-oriented
language.";
    int charPos = sentence2.IndexOf("i");

    string sentence3 = sentence2.Substring(charPos);

    Console.WriteLine(sentence3);
    }


    }
}
$mcs *.cs -out:main.exe
$mono main.exe
```

is an interesting object-oriented language.

The results were not as I had intended. I wanted to create the string starting from the word 'interesting.' However, the word 'is' also starts from the word 'i' and this came before the word 'interesting'. As such the substring was created from the same word. There is a solution to this problem. I will add another alphabet from the word interesting and expect the desired results. Another alphabet from the desired word will add clarity to the program and the compiler will find it easy to locate the desired word.

```
    using System.IO;
    using System;
    namespace MyApplication
    {
```

```
class Program
{
  static void Main(string[] args)
  {
    string sentence2 = " It is an interesting object-oriented
language.";
    int charPos = sentence2.IndexOf("in");

    string sentence3 = sentence2.Substring(charPos);

    Console.WriteLine(sentence3);
  }

}
}
$mcs *.cs -out:main.exe
$mono main.exe
```

interesting object-oriented language.

C# Arrays & Lists

Arrays are created and used to storing multiple values in one
variable instead of declaring individual variables for each value.
You will first have to declare an array and define the type of
variable that you will be filling in. When you have declared the
variable, you need to place the values in a comma-separated list
within the curly braces.

```
using System;
namespace MyApp
{
  class Program1
  {
    static void Main(string[] args)
    {
      string[] fruits = {"guava", "grapefruit", "apple", "banana",
"strawberry", "blueberry", "jackfruit", "dragonfruit", "peach",
"apricot"};
      Console.WriteLine(fruits[0]);
      Console.WriteLine(fruits[3]);
      Console.WriteLine(fruits[1]);
      Console.WriteLine(fruits[6]);
      Console.WriteLine(fruits[8]);
    }
  }
}
$mcs *.cs -out:main.exe
$mono main.exe
guava
banana
grapefruit
jackfruit
peach
```

Take another example in which I will try to access the items that are not in the index. You will receive an error.

```csharp
using System;
namespace MyApp
{
  class Program1
  {
    static void Main(string[] args)
    {
      string[] fruits = {"guava", "grapefruit", "apple", "banana",
"strawberry", "blueberry", "jackfruit", "dragonfruit", "peach",
"apricot"};
      Console.WriteLine(fruits[0]);
      Console.WriteLine(fruits[3]);
      Console.WriteLine(fruits[1]);
      Console.WriteLine(fruits[6]);
      Console.WriteLine(fruits[8]);
      Console.WriteLine(fruits[7]);
      Console.WriteLine(fruits[9]);
      Console.WriteLine(fruits[2]);
      Console.WriteLine(fruits[12]);
    }
  }
}
$mcs *.cs -out:main.exe
$mono main.exe
guava
banana
grapefruit
jackfruit
```

peach

dragonfruit

apricot

apple

Unhandled Exception:

System.IndexOutOfRangeException: Index was outside the bounds of the array.

```
    at MyApp.Program1.Main (System.String[] args) [0x0009a]
    in <da27370ce8d24ef0a5fdcd220b94022f>:0
    [ERROR] FATAL UNHANDLED EXCEPTION:
    System.IndexOutOfRangeException: Index was outside the
    bounds of the array.
    at MyApp.Program1.Main (System.String[] args) [0x0009a]
    in <da27370ce8d24ef0a5fdcd220b94022f>:0
```

You also can change an array element by referring to the index number of the element. See the following example.

```
using System;
namespace MyApp
{
  class Program1
  {
    static void Main(string[] args)
    {
```

```csharp
        string[] fruits = {"guava", "grapefruit", "apple", "banana",
"strawberry", "blueberry", "jackfruit", "dragonfruit", "peach",
"apricot"};
        fruits[0] = "plum";
        Console.WriteLine(fruits[0]);
        fruits[1] = "melon";
        Console.WriteLine(fruits[1]);
        fruits[2] = "watermelon";
        Console.WriteLine(fruits[2]);
        fruits[3] = "mango";
        Console.WriteLine(fruits[3]);
        fruits[4] = "lychee";
        Console.WriteLine(fruits[4]);
        fruits[5] = "tomato";
        Console.WriteLine(fruits[5]);
        fruits[6] = "orange";
        Console.WriteLine(fruits[6]);
        fruits[7] = "fig";
        Console.WriteLine(fruits[7]);
    }
  }
}
```

$mcs *.cs -out:main.exe
$mono main.exe
plum
melon
watermelon
mango

lychee

tomato

orange

fig

Array Length

You can check the length of the array by using the following code. Let's try it.

```
using System;
namespace MyApp
{
  class Program1
  {
    static void Main(string[] args)
    {
      string[] fruits = {"guava", "grapefruit", "apple", "banana",
"strawberry", "blueberry", "jackfruit", "dragonfruit", "peach",
"apricot"};
      Console.WriteLine(fruits.Length);
    }
  }
}
$mcs *.cs -out:main.exe
$mono main.exe
10
```

Array Loop

C# gives you the option of looping through the array elements with a *for* loop. You also can use the Length property for specifying how many times the loop should run. The following example will loop through all elements of fruits array.

```
using System;
namespace MyApp
{
  class Program1
  {
    static void Main(string[] args)
    {
      string[] fruits = {"guava", "grapefruit", "apple", "banana",
"strawberry", "blueberry", "jackfruit", "dragonfruit", "peach",
"apricot"};
      for (int i = 0; i < fruits.Length; i++)
{
  Console.WriteLine(fruits[i]);
}
    }
  }
}
$mcs *.cs -out:main.exe
$mono main.exe
guava
grapefruit
apple
```

banana

strawberry

blueberry

jackfruit

dragonfruit

peach

apricot

If you change the symbol of less than to greater than, you will not have any results.

```csharp
using System;
namespace MyApp
{
  class Program1
  {
    static void Main(string[] args)
    {
      string[] fruits = {"guava", "grapefruit", "apple", "banana",
"strawberry", "blueberry", "jackfruit", "dragonfruit", "peach",
"apricot"};
      for (int i = 50; i > fruits.Length; i++)
{
  Console.WriteLine(fruits[i]);
}
    }
  }
}
```

The result will be an empty page. You also can change the value of i and the looping will be limited. This can be handy in case you create a program for which you want the users to see only a few elements.

```csharp
using System;
using System.Collections.Generic;
namespace MyApp
{
  class Program1
  {
    static void Main(string[] args)
    {
      List<string> fruits = new List<string>();
// add fruits
fruits.Add(" apple ");
fruits.Add(" banana ");
fruits.Add(" orange ");
fruits.Add(" plum ");
fruits.Add(" guava ");
fruits.Add(" melon ");
fruits.Add(" watermelon ");
fruits.Add(" strawberry ");
fruits.Add(" blueberry ");
fruits.Add(" jackfruit ");
fruits.Add(" dragonfruit ");
// now remove the banana
fruits.Remove("banana");
```

```
Console.WriteLine(fruits.Count);
    }
  }
}
$mcs *.cs -out:main.exe
$mono main.exe
11
```

Item Removal

If you want to remove items from a list, you can use another method for the purpose. If you are creating a program in which a vendor sells fruit, you can write in such a way that whenever the vendor sells out a particular fruit, the player will be able to remove the empty cart from the shop by using the index number of the fruit.

```
using System;
using System.Collections.Generic;
namespace MyApp
{
  class Program1
  {
    static void Main(string[] args)
    {
      List<string> fruits = new List<string>();
fruits.Add(" apple ");
fruits.Add(" banana ");
fruits.Add(" orange ");
fruits.Add(" plum ");
```

```
fruits.Add(" guava ");
fruits.Add(" melon ");
fruits.Add(" watermelon ");
fruits.Add(" strawberry ");
fruits.Add(" blueberry ");
fruits.Add(" jackfruit ");
fruits.Add(" dragonfruit ");
fruits.RemoveAt(1);
fruits.RemoveAt(5);
Console.WriteLine(fruits.Count);
    }
  }
}
$mcs *.cs -out:main.exe
$mono main.exe
9
```

C# Lists

C# has been fun to code in and one reason behind this is lists. This post will tell you how you can fill items into a list. You can add, sort or remove different items from a list. C# has indexed lists and like the arrays the index starts at 0. The items are not sorted. While an array has a fixed size, the items in a list can be changed at will, which is why a list is the perfect choice if you don't know the number of items that you must include in it. It is estimated that you can pack up about two million elements in a list if you are operating a 64-bit operating system.

```
using System;
using System.Collections.Generic;

class Program1 {

    // Main Method
    public static void Main(String[] args)
    {

        // I am now creating a List of integers
        List<int> flist = new List<int>();


        // I am here displaying the number
        // of different elements of the List<T>
        Console.WriteLine(flist.Count);
    }
}
$mcs *.cs -out:main.exe
$mono main.exe
0
```

See another example of C# lists. I will use more digits.

```
using System;
using System.Collections.Generic;

class Program1 {
```

```csharp
// Main Method
public static void Main(String[] args)
{

    // I am Creating the List of integers
    List<int> flist = new List<int>();

    // I am now adding the elements in flist
    flist.Add(1);
    flist.Add(2);
    flist.Add(3);
    flist.Add(4);

    Console.WriteLine("The Capacity here Is: " +
flist.Capacity);

    Console.WriteLine("The Count here is: " + flist.Count);

    flist.Add(5);
    flist.Add(6);

    Console.WriteLine("The Capacity here Is: " +
flist.Capacity);

    Console.WriteLine("The Count here Is: " + flist.Count);
}
}
```

$mcs *.cs -out:main.exe
$mono main.exe
The Capacity here Is: 4
The Count here is: 4
The Capacity here Is: 8
The Count here Is: 6

You can check in a list whether a digit is present or not by adding simple method to the code.

```
using System;
using System.Collections.Generic;

class Program1 {

    // Main Method
    public static void Main(String[] args)
    {

        // I am Creating the List of integers
        List<int> flist = new List<int>();

        // I am now adding the elements in flist
        flist.Add(1);
        flist.Add(2);
        flist.Add(3);
        flist.Add(4);
        flist.Add(5);
```

```
flist.Add(6);

Console.WriteLine(flist.Contains(5));

    }
}
```

$mcs *.cs -out:main.exe
$mono main.exe
True

If the digit is not present, the result will be different.

```
using System;
using System.Collections.Generic;

class Program1 {

    // Main Method
    public static void Main(String[] args)
    {

        // I am Creating the List of integers
        List<int> flist = new List<int>();

        // I am now adding the elements in flist
        flist.Add(1) ;
        flist.Add(2) ;
        flist.Add(3) ;
```

```
flist.Add(4) ;
flist.Add(5) ;
flist.Add(6) ;

Console.WriteLine(flist.Contains(50));

    }
}
```
$mcs *.cs -out:main.exe
$mono main.exe
False

Here is another example of list creation by using C#.

```
using System;
using System.Collections.Generic;

class Program1 {

    // This is the Main Method
    public static void Main(String[] args)
    {

        // Mow I am Creating a List<T> of Integers
        List<int> flist = new List<int>();

        // Adding elements to List
        flist.Add(17);
```

```
flist.Add(19);
flist.Add(21);
flist.Add(9);
flist.Add(75);
flist.Add(19);
flist.Add(73);

Console.WriteLine("Take a look the elements present in
the List:\n");

int p = 0;

// Now I am displaying elements
foreach(int k in flist)
{
    Console.Write("We are at Position {0}: ", p);
    Console.WriteLine(k);
    p++;
}

Console.WriteLine(" ");

Console.WriteLine("I am removing the element at the
index 3\n");

flist.RemoveAt(3);

int p1 = 0;
```

```
        foreach(int n in flist)
        {
            Console.Write("now I am at Position {0}: ", p1);
            Console.WriteLine(n);
            p1++;
        }
    }
}
```

$mcs *.cs -out:main.exe
$mono main.exe

Take a look the elements present in the List:

    We are at Position 0: 17
    We are at Position 1: 19
    We are at Position 2: 21
    We are at Position 3: 9
    We are at Position 4: 75
    We are at Position 5: 19
    We are at Position 6: 73

I am removing the element at the index 3

    At Position 0: 17
    At Position 1: 19
    At Position 2: 21
    At Position 3: 75
    At Position 4: 19
    At Position 5: 73

List Creation

You can create a list of fruits and count the numbers by using the following method. See the example below.

```
using System;
using System.Collections.Generic;

class Program1 {

    // This is the Main Method
    public static void Main(String[] args)
    {

        List<string> fruit = new List<string>();
// add fruits
        fruit.Add("Apple") ;
        fruit.Add("Banana") ;
        fruit.Add("Orange") ;
        fruit.Add("Peach") ;
        fruit.Add("Guava") ;
        fruit.Add("Melon") ;
        fruit.Add("Watermelon") ;
        fruit.Add("Lychee") ;
        fruit.Add("Strawberry") ;
        fruit.Add("Blueberry") ;
        fruit.Add("Raspberry") ;
        fruit.Add("Dragonfruit") ;
        fruit.Add("Jackfruit") ;
```

```
        fruit.Add("Coconut") ;
        fruit.Add("Banana") ;
// now remove the banana
        Console.WriteLine(fruit.Count);
        }
    }
```

$mcs *.cs -out:main.exe
$mono main.exe
15

Item Removal

If you intend to remove items from the list, there is a simple method
to do that. See the following example.

```
using System;
using System.Collections.Generic;

class Program1 {

    // This is the Main Method
    public static void Main(String[] args)
    {

        List<string> fruit = new List<string>();
// add fruits
        fruit.Add("Apple") ;
        fruit.Add("Banana") ;
        fruit.Add("Orange") ;
```

```
        fruit.Add("Peach") ;
        fruit.Add("Guava") ;
        fruit.Add("Melon") ;
        fruit.Add("Watermelon") ;
        fruit.Add("Lychee") ;
        fruit.Add("Strawberry") ;
        fruit.Add("Blueberry") ;
        fruit.Add("Raspberry") ;
        fruit.Add("Dragonfruit") ;
        fruit.Add("Jackfruit") ;
        fruit.Add("Coconut") ;
        fruit.Add("Banana") ;
// now remove the banana
        fruit.Remove("Banana");
        Console.WriteLine(fruit.Count);
        }
    }
```

$mcs *.cs -out:main.exe
$mono main.exe
14

You can remove the items by using the index number. The method for the purpose is called RemoveAt().

```
    using System;
    using System.Collections.Generic;


    class Program1 {
```

```csharp
// This is the Main Method
public static void Main(String[] args)
{

    List<string> fruit = new List<string>();
// add fruits
    fruit.Add("Apple") ;
    fruit.Add("Banana") ;
    fruit.Add("Orange") ;
    fruit.Add("Peach") ;
    fruit.Add("Guava") ;
    fruit.Add("Melon") ;
    fruit.Add("Watermelon") ;
    fruit.Add("Lychee") ;
    fruit.Add("Strawberry") ;
    fruit.Add("Blueberry") ;
    fruit.Add("Raspberry") ;
    fruit.Add("Dragonfruit") ;
    fruit.Add("Jackfruit") ;
    fruit.Add("Coconut") ;
    fruit.Add("Banana") ;
// now remove the banana
    fruit.RemoveAt(2);
    Console.WriteLine(fruit.Count);
    }
}
$mcs *.cs -out:main.exe
```

$mono main.exe

14

Concatenation

You also can combine two lists and count their number by using the AddRange method.

```
using System;
using System.Collections.Generic;
namespace MyApp
{
  class Program1
  {
    static void Main(string[] args)
    {
      List<string> fruits = new List<string>();
fruits.Add(" apple ");
fruits.Add(" banana ");
fruits.Add(" orange ");
fruits.Add(" plum ");
fruits.Add(" guava ");
List<string> fruits2 = new List<string>();
fruits2.Add(" melon ");
fruits2.Add(" watermelon ");
fruits2.Add(" strawberry ");
fruits2.Add(" blueberry ");
fruits2.Add(" jackfruit ");
fruits2.Add(" dragonfruit ");
```

```
fruits.AddRange(fruits2);
Console.WriteLine(fruits.Count);
    }
  }
}
$mcs *.cs -out:main.exe
$mono main.exe
11
```

Chapter Three

C# Conditionals

C# conditional statements generally are used when you have to execute or simply test a particular action depending on a specific condition. C# allows programmers to test multiple conditions. You can apply certain logical conditions from mathematics. You can test conditions like less than, less than or equal to, equal to, greater than, greater than or equal to, and not equal to. These conditions can be used to perform different actions to make different decisions. Just like other programming languages C# can test a number of conditions like if, else if, else and switch.

Let's try a simple condition using the *if* condition. The condition will be true if the number before the greater than sign is greater than 18. If not, the condition will be false.

```
using System.IO;
using System;
class Program1
{
    static void Main()
    {
```

```
    if (50 > 18)
    {
       Console.WriteLine("The Number 50 is greater than 20");
    }
  }
}
$mcs *.cs -out:main.exe
$mono main.exe
The Number 50 is greater than 20
```

Now I will change the values and see what happens. If we put a lower number before the greater than sign, the result will be a compilation error.

```
using System.IO;
using System;
class Program1
{
   static void Main()
   {
      if (50 > 60)
      {
         Console.WriteLine("The Number 50 is greater than 60");
      }
   }
}
$mcs *.cs -out:main.exe
Compilation succeeded - 1 warning(s)
```

main.cs(10,9): warning CS0162: Unreachable code detected

$mono main.exe

In the following examples, I will test and see the results of other conditions I have talked about at the start of the topic. The first on the line is the less than sign. It will show a simple message that a particular number is less than the other one. See the following example. All you need to do is to change the greater than sign to less than, and also change the statement.

```
using System.IO;
using System;
class Program1
{
    static void Main()
    {
        if (50 < 60)
        {
            Console.WriteLine("The Number 50 is less than 60");
        }
    }
}
$mcs *.cs -out:main.exe
$mono main.exe
The Number 50 is less than 60
```

The next is the less than or equal to sign. I will also change the statement that will be displayed to the user.

```
using System.IO;
using System;
class Program1
{
    static void Main()
    {
        if (60 <= 60)
        {
            Console.WriteLine("The Number 50 is less than or equal to 60");
        }
    }
}
$mcs *.cs -out:main.exe
$mono main.exe
The Number 50 is less than or equal to 60
```

The conditional is the 'greater than' or 'equal to' option. I will change the sign and the statement that will be printed by the compiler. See how it works.

```
using System.IO;
using System;
class Program1
{
    static void Main()
    {
        if (70 >= 60)
```

```
        {
        Console.WriteLine("The Number 70 is less than or equal
to 60");
        }
    }
}
$mcs *.cs -out:main.exe
$mono main.exe
The Number 70 is less than or equal to 60
```

In the next code snippet, I will make sure that the two numbers are equal.

```
using System.IO;
using System;
class Program1
{
    static void Main()
    {
        if (60 >= 60)
        {
        Console.WriteLine("The Number 60 is less than or equal
to 60");
        }
    }
}
$mcs *.cs -out:main.exe
$mono main.exe
The Number 60 is less than or equal to 60
```

There is another option that tells whether a number is equal to a number or not. It checks the condition and displays the result in the form of a statement. The sign you will use for the purpose is ==. I will replace the sign and change the statement to put this to work.

```
using System.IO;
using System;
class Program1
{
    static void Main()
    {
        if (60 == 60)
        {
            Console.WriteLine("The Number 60 is equal to 60");
        }
    }
}
$mcs *.cs -out:main.exe
$mono main.exe
The Number 60 is equal to 60
```

There is a separate operator to check if two numbers are unequal or not. You will have to replace the == sign with != and check out the results. See the following code snippet.

```
using System.IO;
using System;
class Program1
{
```

```
static void Main()
{
    if (70 != 60)
    {
        Console.WriteLine("The Number 70 is not equal to 60");
    }
}
}
$mcs *.cs -out:main.exe
$mono main.exe
The Number 70 is not equal to 60
```

Now that we have tested all the operators that you will have to use while writing conditional statements, you can move on to practicing the first conditional statement that is the *if* statement. You have seen the simplest use of the *if* statement. One thing to keep in mind is that you always have to write *if* in lowercase letters. If you write it in uppercase letters, it will generate an error. Let's see how the error will look like if you change the case of letters.

```
using System.IO;
using System;
class Program1
{
    static void Main()
    {
        If (70 != 60)
        {
```

```
      Console.WriteLine("The Number 70 is not equal to 60");
   }
   }
}
$mcs *.cs -out:main.exe
Compilation failed: 1 error(s), 0 warnings
main.cs(9,6): error CS1525: Unexpected symbol `{'
```

Now I will change both letters to uppercase.

```
using System.IO;
using System;
class Program1
{
   static void Main()
   {
      IF (70 != 60)
      {
      Console.WriteLine("The Number 70 is not equal to 60");
      }
      }
}
$mcs *.cs -out:main.exe
Compilation failed: 1 error(s), 0 warnings
main.cs(9,6): error CS1525: Unexpected symbol `{'
```

You can see that in both attempts, the compilation failed and we had an error. One of the most interesting features of the conditional statements is that it allows you to test different variables and the condition between them. I will fill in the program with two variables a and b, and then I will test them using different conditions that I have already mentioned.

```
using System.IO;
using System;
class Program1
{
    static void Main()
    {
        int a = 30;
        int b = 28;
        if (a > b)
        {
            Console.WriteLine("The variable a is greater than b.");
        }
    }
}
$mcs *.cs -out:main.exe
$mono main.exe
The variable a is greater than b.
```

In the next code snippet, I will use the >= operator.

```
using System.IO;
using System;
class Program1
{
    static void Main()
    {
```

```
    int a = 30;
    int b = 28;
    if (a >= b)
    {
    Console.WriteLine("The variable a is greater than b.");
    }
  }
}
```
$mcs *.cs -out:main.exe

$mono main.exe

The variable a is greater than b.

In the next example, I will use the less than operator on the same equation and the result will be an error.

```
using System.IO;
using System;
class Program1
{
    static void Main()
    {
      int a = 30;
      int b = 28;
      if (a < b)
      {
      Console.WriteLine("The variable a is greater than b.");
      }
    }
```

```
}
```

The result will be empty or an error as the compiler will be unable to process the information. In the above examples, I have used two variables a and b to test if a is greater than b by using the operator >. Then I wrote a statement that the program printed after testing the condition.

The Else Statement

You can use the else statement for specifying a certain block of code that you can execute if the condition stands false. There are two blocks of code in the if-else statement. If the condition is true, the first block of code executed. If the condition is false, the second block of code is executed. In the following example, I will write a simple if-else statement that reads the time, test the condition and displays a greetings message for the user. You can use this simple program in your office or the reception of your business.

```
using System;
using System.Collections.Generic;
namespace MyApp
{
  class Program1
  {
    static void Main(string[] args)
    {
      int time = 15;
if (time < 16)
{
  Console.WriteLine("Good day.");
}
else
{
  Console.WriteLine("Good evening.");
}
    }
  }
}
$mcs *.cs -out:main.exe
$mono main.exe
Good day.
```

In this example, the second block of code is executed because the condition turned out to be false. In the next block of code, I will test the first block of code.

```
using System;
using System.Collections.Generic;
namespace MyApp
{
  class Program1
  {
    static void Main(string[] args)
    {
      int time = 18;
if (time < 16)
{
  Console.WriteLine("Good day.");
}
else
{
  Console.WriteLine("Good evening.");
}
    }
  }
}
$mcs *.cs -out:main.exe
$mono main.exe
Good evening.
```

The Else If Statement

The else if statement is used for specifying a new condition if the first block of code is false. In this conditional test, the first block of code is executed if the condition stands true. If the first condition is false, the compiler moves on to the next block of code to test the condition. The second block is executed and if the condition is true, the program stops there. If the second condition is also false, the condition moves on to the third block of code and executes it. In the following example, I will set up three conditionals with an else if at the end of the code to test how the three blocks of code of work.

```
using System;
namespace MyApp
{
  class Program1
  {
    static void Main(string[] args)
    {
      int time = 24;
      if (time < 8)
      {
        Console.WriteLine("Good morning. Hope you are doing well!");
      }
      else if (time < 16)
      {
        Console.WriteLine("Good day. Hope you are doing well!");
```

```
    }
    else
    {
        Console.WriteLine("Good evening. Hope you are doing
well!");
    }
  }
 }
}
```

$mcs *.cs -out:main.exe
$mono main.exe

Good evening. Hope you are doing well!

In the above example you can see that 24 is greater than 8 so the first condition is false. The next condition in the else if statement also stands False so that we can move on to the else condition since the first two conditions are false. The message we get on the screen is Good evening. Hope you are doing well! Let's see change the time and see which condition stands true and how it affects the code.

```
using System;
namespace MyApp
{
  class Program1
  {
    static void Main(string[] args)
    {
      int time = 20;
```

```
    if (time < 21)
    {
    Console.WriteLine("Good morning. Hope you are doing
well!");
    }
    else if (time < 16)
    {
    Console.WriteLine("Good day. Hope you are doing
well!");
    }
    else
    {
    Console.WriteLine("Good evening. Hope you are doing
well!");
    }
    }
  }
}
```

$mcs *.cs -out:main.exe
$mono main.exe

Good morning. Hope you are doing well!

I have changed the time in the first condition so that the first condition stands true and we get the Good morning message as a result. Let's further change the value and see which condition stands true as a result.

```
using System;
namespace MyApp
{
```

```csharp
class Program1
{
    static void Main(string[] args)
    {
        int time = 15;
        if (time < 8)
        {
            Console.WriteLine("Good morning. Hope you are doing well!");
        }
        else if (time < 16)
        {
            Console.WriteLine("Good day. Hope you are doing well!");
        }
        else
        {
            Console.WriteLine("Good evening. Hope you are doing well!");
        }
    }
}
```
$mcs *.cs -out:main.exe
$mono main.exe
Good day. Hope you are doing well!

In this code snippet, the second condition stands true and the code is executed displaying the Good day message.

Chapter Four

Interactive Programming

C# is an interesting language when it comes to writing a program that welcomes user input. You have read about C# variables. These variables are used to store different types of input that is entered by different users. This chapter will walk you through the process of accepting input from users, storing data in a variable and then displaying different messages to the users. If you want to display messages to users, you can use the Write() or WriteLine() methods that are built-in in the C# language. Although the function of both methods is the same, the major difference between the two is that they WriteLine() brings the cursor down to the next line after it has displayed the message. The other method doesn't give any such privilege to the users.

User Input

You have learned how to write Console.WriteLine() to display different types of output in a program. There is another feature in C# that you can use to read input by a user. I will be using Console.ReadLine() to receive the user input. This feature is very helpful for creating a program that needs users to enter the input. The input is then stored in a variable. The program will then print the value of the variable.

```
using System;
namespace MyApp
{
  class Program1
  {
    static void Main(string[] args)
    {
    // You are required to type the username and then press enter
    Console.WriteLine("Please Enter the username: Jack");
    // Now I will create a variable to store user input from your keyboard
```

```
    string usrName = Console.ReadLine();
    // Now I will print the value of this newly created variable,
which will display this input value
    Console.WriteLine("The desired username is: " +
usrName);
  }
 }
}
```

$mcs *.cs -out:main.exe
$mono main.exe
Please Enter the username: Jack
The desired username is:

Numerical Input

In the above program, the input type was string. The Console.ReadLine() will return a string. As I have specified it, I will not be able to get value from another data type such as int. You can use the following method to receive numerical input.

```
using System;
namespace MyApp
{
  class Program1
  {
    static void Main(string[] args)
    {
      Console.WriteLine("You are required to enter your age:");
      int yourage = Convert.ToInt32(Console.ReadLine());
```

```
        Console.WriteLine("Your age is: " + yourage);
    }
  }
}
```

$mcs *.cs -out:main.exe

$mono main.exe

You are required to enter your age: 56

Your age is: 0

C# Switch Statement

By using a switch statement, you can test a variable against values that you have allocated to a list. Values are dubbed as cases, and the variable that is switched on is verified for switch case. There are some rules that you must follow when you are writing switch statements.

The expression in a switch statement ought to be an integral type. There is no limit to the number of cases in a switch. You should make sure to insert a colon to the end of each case. The constant-expression and variable must be of the same data type in a switch. If the variable is equal to the case, the execution will continue to the point you have included the break statement in the code. The break statement terminates the switch. If you have forgotten to include a break statement, you will see a compilation error. You must include a default case at the end of the switch statement.

```
    using System.IO;
    using System;
```

```csharp
class Program
{
    static void Main()
    {
        int day = 1;
switch (day)
{
  case 1:
    Console.WriteLine("We will start construction of the office
on Monday");
    break;
  case 2:
    Console.WriteLine("We will start construction of the office
on Tuesday");
    break;
  case 3:
    Console.WriteLine("We will start construction of the office
on Wednesday");
    break;
  case 4:
    Console.WriteLine("We will start construction of the office
on Thursday");
    break;
  case 5:
    Console.WriteLine("We will start construction of the office
on Friday");
    break;
  case 6:
```

```
    Console.WriteLine("We will start construction of the office
on Saturday");
    break;
  case 7:
    Console.WriteLine("We will start construction of the office
on Sunday");
    break;
}
    }
}
```
$mcs *.cs -out:main.exe
$mono main.exe
We will start construction of the office on Monday

I will enter different values to see how the switch statement executes different blocks of code from the program.

```
using System.IO;
using System;
class Program1
{
    static void Main()
    {
      int day = 3;
switch (day)
{
  case 1:
```

```csharp
        Console.WriteLine("We will start construction of the office on Monday");
        break;
    case 2:
        Console.WriteLine("We will start construction of the office on Tuesday");
        break;
    case 3:
        Console.WriteLine("We will start construction of the office on Wednesday");
        break;
    case 4:
        Console.WriteLine("We will start construction of the office on Thursday");
        break;
    case 5:
        Console.WriteLine("We will start construction of the office on Friday");
        break;
    case 6:
        Console.WriteLine("We will start construction of the office on Saturday");
        break;
    case 7:
        Console.WriteLine("We will start construction of the office on Sunday");
        break;
}
```

```
    }
}
```

$mcs *.cs -out:main.exe

$mono main.exe

We will start construction of the office on Wednesday

I will try a different value in the next example.

```
using System.IO;
using System;
class Program1
{
    static void Main()
    {
        int day = 5;
switch (day)
{
  case 1:
    Console.WriteLine("We will start construction of the office
on Monday");
    break;
  case 2:
    Console.WriteLine("We will start construction of the office
on Tuesday");
    break;
  case 3:
    Console.WriteLine("We will start construction of the office
on Wednesday");
```

84

```
    break;
  case 4:
    Console.WriteLine("We will start construction of the office
on Thursday");
    break;
  case 5:
    Console.WriteLine("We will start construction of the office
on Friday");
    break;
  case 6:
    Console.WriteLine("We will start construction of the office
on Saturday");
    break;
  case 7:
    Console.WriteLine("We will start construction of the office
on Sunday");
    break;
}
  }
}
```

$mcs *.cs -out:main.exe
$mono main.exe
We will start construction of the office on Friday

There is another example that will further explain how to write a switch statement and how to get the results you want.

```
using System.IO;
```

```csharp
using System;
class Program1
{
    static void Main()
    {
        int day = 7;
switch (day)
{
  case 1:
    Console.WriteLine("We will start construction of the office
on Monday");
    break;
  case 2:
    Console.WriteLine("We will start construction of the office
on Tuesday");
    break;
  case 3:
    Console.WriteLine("We will start construction of the office
on Wednesday");
    break;
  case 4:
    Console.WriteLine("We will start construction of the office
on Thursday");
    break;
  case 5:
    Console.WriteLine("We will start construction of the office
on Friday");
    break;
```

```
   case 6:
   Console.WriteLine("We will start construction of the office
on Saturday");
   break;
   case 7:
   Console.WriteLine("We will start construction of the office
on Sunday");
   break;
}
   }
}
```

$mcs *.cs -out:main.exe
$mono main.exe
We will start construction of the office on Sunday

Let me try an even number in the program. It will work as well as an odd number does.

```
using System.IO;
using System;
class Program1
{
   static void Main()
   {
     int day = 4;
switch (day)
{
   case 1:
```

```csharp
        Console.WriteLine("We will start construction of the office on Monday");
        break;
    case 2:
        Console.WriteLine("We will start construction of the office on Tuesday");
        break;
    case 3:
        Console.WriteLine("We will start construction of the office on Wednesday");
        break;
    case 4:
        Console.WriteLine("We will start construction of the office on Thursday");
        break;
    case 5:
        Console.WriteLine("We will start construction of the office on Friday");
        break;
    case 6:
        Console.WriteLine("We will start construction of the office on Saturday");
        break;
    case 7:
        Console.WriteLine("We will start construction of the office on Sunday");
        break;
}
```

```
        }
    }
```

$mcs *.cs -out:main.exe

$mono main.exe

We will start construction of the office on Thursday

The only thing you need to keep in mind is the number of blocks of code that you have in your program. If you forget the number and enter something that exceeds the number of code blocks, the result will be empty. Be careful because C# is a compiled language, which makes it hard to spot an error or a missing line of code.

```csharp
using System.IO;
using System;
class Program1
{
    static void Main()
    {
        int day = 9;
switch (day)
{
  case 1:
    Console.WriteLine("We will start construction of the office
on Monday");
    break;
  case 2:
    Console.WriteLine("We will start construction of the office
on Tuesday");
```

```
      break;
   case 3:
   Console.WriteLine("We will start construction of the office
on Wednesday");
      break;
   case 4:
   Console.WriteLine("We will start construction of the office
on Thursday");
      break;
   case 5:
   Console.WriteLine("We will start construction of the office
on Friday");
      break;
   case 6:
   Console.WriteLine("We will start construction of the office
on Saturday");
      break;
   case 7:
   Console.WriteLine("We will start construction of the office
on Sunday");
      break;
}
   }
}
$mcs *.cs -out:main.exe
$mono main.exe
```

The Break Keyword

The break keyword terminates the switch statement or loop statement. The loop doesn't stop until it stumbles upon a break statement. If you are running two loops in your program and the break keyword is placed inside the inner loop, the break keyword will only terminate the inner loop. There will be no effect on the outer loop.

```
using System.IO;
using System;
class Program1
{
    static void Main()
    {
        int day = 1;
switch (day)
{
  case 1:
    Console.WriteLine("We will start construction of the office on Monday");
    break;
  case 2:
    Console.WriteLine("We will start construction of the office on Tuesday");
    break;
  case 3:
    Console.WriteLine("We will start construction of the office on Wednesday");
```

```
        break;
    case 4:
    Console.WriteLine("We will start construction of the office
on Thursday");
        break;
        default:
    case 5:
    Console.WriteLine("We will start construction of the office
on Friday");
        break;
    case 6:
    Console.WriteLine("We will start construction of the office
on Saturday");
        break;
    case 7:
    Console.WriteLine("We will start construction of the office
on Sunday");
        break;
}
    }
}
```

$mcs *.cs -out:main.exe

$mono main.exe

We will start construction of the office on Monday

Now I will change the value of the int keyword.

using System.IO;

```
using System;
class Program1
{
    static void Main()
    {
        int day = 15;
switch (day)
{
  case 1:
    Console.WriteLine("We will start construction of the office
on Monday");
    break;
  case 2:
    Console.WriteLine("We will start construction of the office
on Tuesday");
    break;
  case 3:
    Console.WriteLine("We will start construction of the office
on Wednesday");
    break;
  case 4:
    Console.WriteLine("We will start construction of the office
on Thursday");
    break;
    default:
  case 5:
    Console.WriteLine("We will start construction of the office
on Friday");
```

```
    break;
  case 6:
    Console.WriteLine("We will start construction of the office
on Saturday");
    break;
  case 7:
    Console.WriteLine("We will start construction of the office
on Sunday");
    break;
}
  }
}
```

$mcs *.cs -out:main.exe

$mono main.exe

We will start construction of the office on Friday

You can see that I had entered 15 as the value but still I got the default result from the program.

Chapter Five

C# Loops

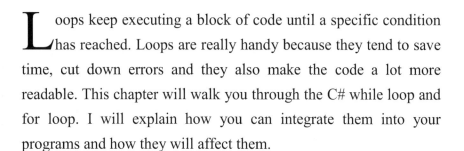

Loops keep executing a block of code until a specific condition has reached. Loops are really handy because they tend to save time, cut down errors and they also make the code a lot more readable. This chapter will walk you through the C# while loop and for loop. I will explain how you can integrate them into your programs and how they will affect them.

C# While Loop

The while loop tends to loop through a block of code until a condition stands true. In the following example, the code will keep running, until the condition is true. The while loop initiates with the while keyword and it ought to include a Boolean conditional expression within brackets that would return false or true. It also executes a code block until a specific conditional expression returns false.

```
using System.IO;
using System;
```

```
class Program1
{
    static void Main()
    {
        int x = 0; // this is the initialization
while (x < 50) // here is the condition
{
    Console.WriteLine("x = {0}", x);
    x++; // this is the increment
    }
    }
}
```
$mcs *.cs -out:main.exe
$mono main.exe
x = 0
x = 1
x = 2
x = 3
x = 4
x = 5
x = 6
x = 7
x = 8
x = 9
x = 10
x = 11
x = 12
x = 13

x = 14

x = 15

x = 16

x = 17

x = 18

x = 19

x = 20

x = 21

x = 22

x = 23

x = 24

x = 25

x = 26

x = 27

x = 28

x = 29

x = 30

x = 31

x = 32

x = 33

x = 34

x = 35

x = 36

x = 37

x = 38

x = 39

x = 40

x = 41

x = 42

x = 43

x = 44

x = 45

x = 46

x = 47

x = 48

x = 49

If we change the condition, the loop will stop at a previous or a later stage. I will set it at 25 in the following example.

```csharp
using System.IO;
using System;
class Program1
{
    static void Main()
    {
      int x = 0; // this is the initialization
while (x < 25) // here is the condition
{
    Console.WriteLine("x = {0}", x);
    x++; // this is the increment
    }
    }
}
$mcs *.cs -out:main.exe
$mono main.exe
```

x = 0

x = 1

x = 2

x = 3

x = 4

x = 5

x = 6

x = 7

x = 8

x = 9

x = 10

x = 11

x = 12

x = 13

x = 14

x = 15

x = 16

x = 17

x = 18

x = 19

x = 20

x = 21

x = 22

x = 23

x = 24

If we change the operator from less than to greater than, the results will drastically change. There will be a need to add the break keyword to stop the loop.

```
using System.IO;
using System;
class Program1
{
    static void Main()
    {
        int x = 0; // this is the initialization
while (true) // here is the condition
{
    Console.WriteLine("x = {0}", x);
    x++; // this is the increment

    if(x > 50)
    break;
    }
    }
}
$mcs *.cs -out:main.exe
$mono main.exe
x = 0
x = 1
x = 2
x = 3
x = 4
```

$x = 5$

$x = 6$

$x = 7$

$x = 8$

$x = 9$

$x = 10$

$x = 11$

$x = 12$

$x = 13$

$x = 14$

$x = 15$

$x = 16$

$x = 17$

$x = 18$

$x = 19$

$x = 20$

$x = 21$

$x = 22$

$x = 23$

$x = 24$

$x = 25$

$x = 26$

$x = 27$

$x = 28$

$x = 29$

$x = 30$

$x = 31$

$x = 32$

x = 33

x = 34

x = 35

x = 36

x = 37

x = 38

x = 39

x = 40

x = 41

x = 42

x = 43

x = 44

x = 45

x = 46

x = 47

x = 48

x = 49

x = 50

The following is an example of an infinite while loop.

```
using System.IO;
using System;
class Program1
{
    static void Main()
    {
        int x = 0; // this is the initialization
```

```
while (x > 0) // here is the condition
{
    Console.WriteLine("x = {0}", x);
    x++; // this is the increment



    }
    }
}
```
$mcs *.cs -out:main.exe
$mono main.exe

C# Nested While Loop

C# allows loops in another while loop as is displayed below. However, it is not recommended that you use nested while loop as it would be hard to debug and maintain as well.

```
using System.IO;
using System;
class Program1
{
    static void Main()
    {
        int x = 0, y = 1;
    while (x < 30)
    {
        Console.WriteLine("x = {0}", x);
        x++;
```

```csharp
    while (y < 30)
    {
        Console.WriteLine("y = {0}", y);
        y++;
    }
}




    }
    }
```

$mcs *.cs -out:main.exe

$mono main.exe

x = 0

y = 1

y = 2

y = 3

y = 4

y = 5

y = 6

y = 7

y = 8

y = 9

y = 10

y = 11

y = 12

y = 13

y = 14

y = 15

y = 16

y = 17

y = 18

y = 19

y = 20

y = 21

y = 22

y = 23

y = 24

y = 25

y = 26

y = 27

y = 28

y = 29

x = 1

x = 2

x = 3

x = 4

x = 5

x = 6

x = 7

x = 8

x = 9

x = 10

x = 11

x = 12

x = 13

x = 14

x = 15
x = 16
x = 17
x = 18
x = 19
x = 20
x = 21
x = 22
x = 23
x = 24
x = 25
x = 26
x = 27
x = 28
x = 29

The Do-While Loop

The do-while is similar to a simple while loop except it tends to execute the block of code once. It starts with the do keyword followed by another block of code, a Boolean expression and the while keyword. The do-while keyword loop will stop execution exits when a Boolean condition evaluates to false.

```
using System.IO;
using System;
class Program1
{
    static void Main()
```

```
    {
        int x = 0;
do
{
    Console.WriteLine("x = {0}", x);
    x++;
} while (x < 40);
    }
}
```

$mcs *.cs -out:main.exe

$mono main.exe

x = 0

x = 1

x = 2

x = 3

x = 4

x = 5

x = 6

x = 7

x = 8

x = 9

x = 10

x = 11

x = 12

x = 13

x = 14

x = 15

x = 16

x = 17

x = 18

x = 19

x = 20

x = 21

x = 22

x = 23

x = 24

x = 25

x = 26

x = 27

x = 28

x = 29

x = 30

x = 31

x = 32

x = 33

x = 34

x = 35

x = 36

x = 37

x = 38

x = 39

You ought to specify the initialization from the loop and also specify the increment or decrement counter within the do-while loop. You will be using the break or return keywords to exit out of the do-while loop.

```csharp
using System.IO;
using System;
class Program1
{
    static void Main()
    {
        int x = 0;
do
{
    Console.WriteLine("x = {0}", x);
    x++;

    if (x > 40)
        break;
} while (x < 90);
    }
}
```

$mcs *.cs -out:main.exe
$mono main.exe

x = 0
x = 1
x = 2
x = 3
x = 4
x = 5
x = 6
x = 7
x = 8

x = 9

x = 10

x = 11

x = 12

x = 13

x = 14

x = 15

x = 16

x = 17

x = 18

x = 19

x = 20

x = 21

x = 22

x = 23

x = 24

x = 25

x = 26

x = 27

x = 28

x = 29

x = 30

x = 31

x = 32

x = 33

x = 34

x = 35

x = 36

x = 37
x = 38
x = 39
x = 40

C# Nested-do-while Loop

You also can nest a do-while loop in another do-while loop. This sounds a little bit complicating but, in practice, it is quite easier to do.

```
using System.IO;
using System;
class Program1
{
   static void Main()
   {
     int x = 0;
do
{
   Console.WriteLine("The value of x is as follows: {0}", x);
   int y = x;
   x++;

   do
   {
      Console.WriteLine("The value of y is as follows: {0}",
y);
      y++;
```

```
    } while (y < 30);
} while (x < 40);
    }
}
```

$mcs *.cs -out:main.exe

$mono main.exe

The value of x is as follows: 0

The value of y is as follows: 0

The value of y is as follows: 1

The value of y is as follows: 2

The value of y is as follows: 3

The value of y is as follows: 4

The value of y is as follows: 5

The value of y is as follows: 6

The value of y is as follows: 7

The value of y is as follows: 8

The value of y is as follows: 9

The value of y is as follows: 10

The value of y is as follows: 11

The value of y is as follows: 12

The value of y is as follows: 13

The value of y is as follows: 14

The value of y is as follows: 15

The value of y is as follows: 16

The value of y is as follows: 17

The value of y is as follows: 18

The value of y is as follows: 19

The value of y is as follows: 20

The value of y is as follows: 21
The value of y is as follows: 22
The value of y is as follows: 23
The value of y is as follows: 24
The value of y is as follows: 25
The value of y is as follows: 26
The value of y is as follows: 27
The value of y is as follows: 28
The value of y is as follows: 29
The value of x is as follows: 1
The value of y is as follows: 1
The value of y is as follows: 2
The value of y is as follows: 3
The value of y is as follows: 4
The value of y is as follows: 5
The value of y is as follows: 6
The value of y is as follows: 7
The value of y is as follows: 8
The value of y is as follows: 9
The value of y is as follows: 10
The value of y is as follows: 11
The value of y is as follows: 12
The value of y is as follows: 13
The value of y is as follows: 14
The value of y is as follows: 15
The value of y is as follows: 16
The value of y is as follows: 17
The value of y is as follows: 18

The value of y is as follows: 19
The value of y is as follows: 20
The value of y is as follows: 21
The value of y is as follows: 22
The value of y is as follows: 23
The value of y is as follows: 24
The value of y is as follows: 25
The value of y is as follows: 26
The value of y is as follows: 27
The value of y is as follows: 28
The value of y is as follows: 29
The value of x is as follows: 2
The value of y is as follows: 2
The value of y is as follows: 3
The value of y is as follows: 4
The value of y is as follows: 5
The value of y is as follows: 6
The value of y is as follows: 7
The value of y is as follows: 8
The value of y is as follows: 9
The value of y is as follows: 10
The value of y is as follows: 11
The value of y is as follows: 12
The value of y is as follows: 13
The value of y is as follows: 14
The value of y is as follows: 15
The value of y is as follows: 16
The value of y is as follows: 17

The value of y is as follows: 18

The value of y is as follows: 19

The value of y is as follows: 20

The value of y is as follows: 21

The value of y is as follows: 22

The value of y is as follows: 23

The value of y is as follows: 24

The value of y is as follows: 25

The value of y is as follows: 26

The value of y is as follows: 27

The value of y is as follows: 28

The value of y is as follows: 29

The value of x is as follows: 3

The value of y is as follows: 3

The value of y is as follows: 4

The value of y is as follows: 5

The value of y is as follows: 6

The value of y is as follows: 7

The value of y is as follows: 8

The value of y is as follows: 9

The value of y is as follows: 10

The value of y is as follows: 11

The value of y is as follows: 12

The value of y is as follows: 13

The value of y is as follows: 14

The value of y is as follows: 15

The value of y is as follows: 16

The value of y is as follows: 17

The value of y is as follows: 18

The value of y is as follows: 19

The value of y is as follows: 20

The value of y is as follows: 21

The value of y is as follows: 22

The value of y is as follows: 23

The value of y is as follows: 24

The value of y is as follows: 25

The value of y is as follows: 26

The value of y is as follows: 27

The value of y is as follows: 28

The value of y is as follows: 29

The value of x is as follows: 4

The value of y is as follows: 4

The value of y is as follows: 5

The value of y is as follows: 6

The value of y is as follows: 7

The value of y is as follows: 8

The value of y is as follows: 9

The value of y is as follows: 10

The value of y is as follows: 11

The value of y is as follows: 12

The value of y is as follows: 13

The value of y is as follows: 14

The value of y is as follows: 15

The value of y is as follows: 16

The value of y is as follows: 17

The value of y is as follows: 18

The value of y is as follows: 19
The value of y is as follows: 20
The value of y is as follows: 21
The value of y is as follows: 22
The value of y is as follows: 23
The value of y is as follows: 24
The value of y is as follows: 25
The value of y is as follows: 26
The value of y is as follows: 27
The value of y is as follows: 28
The value of y is as follows: 29
The value of x is as follows: 5
The value of y is as follows: 5
The value of y is as follows: 6
The value of y is as follows: 7
The value of y is as follows: 8
The value of y is as follows: 9
The value of y is as follows: 10
The value of y is as follows: 11
The value of y is as follows: 12
The value of y is as follows: 13
The value of y is as follows: 14
The value of y is as follows: 15
The value of y is as follows: 16
The value of y is as follows: 17
The value of y is as follows: 18
The value of y is as follows: 19
The value of y is as follows: 20

The value of y is as follows: 21
The value of y is as follows: 22
The value of y is as follows: 23
The value of y is as follows: 24
The value of y is as follows: 25
The value of y is as follows: 26
The value of y is as follows: 27
The value of y is as follows: 28
The value of y is as follows: 29
The value of x is as follows: 6
The value of y is as follows: 6
The value of y is as follows: 7
The value of y is as follows: 8
The value of y is as follows: 9
The value of y is as follows: 10
The value of y is as follows: 11
The value of y is as follows: 12
The value of y is as follows: 13
The value of y is as follows: 14
The value of y is as follows: 15
The value of y is as follows: 16
The value of y is as follows: 17
The value of y is as follows: 18
The value of y is as follows: 19
The value of y is as follows: 20
The value of y is as follows: 21
The value of y is as follows: 22
The value of y is as follows: 23

The value of y is as follows: 24

The value of y is as follows: 25

The value of y is as follows: 26

The value of y is as follows: 27

The value of y is as follows: 28

The value of y is as follows: 29

The nested do-while loop is quite interesting because of the fact that the second loop iterates through the first one. The x integer had 7 as a value so for each number of x, the first loop iterated around 30 times as 30 was the value of y. You can copy the code and paste it in a compiler. Change the value of x and you will realize how it will react. If you set the value of x at 100, the first do-while loop will iterate through for each of the 100 values of x. It is amazing.

C# For Loop

When you exactly know how many times you need to loop through a certain block of code, you should run a for loop. Usually, there are three statements in a for loop. The first statement gets executed once before the execution of the block of code. The second statement tends to define the condition for the execution of the block of code. The third statement gets executed after the block of code gets executed.

```
using System.IO;
using System;
class Program1
{
```

```
static void Main()
  {
    for (int x = 50; x < 65; x++)
{
  Console.WriteLine(x);
}
    }
}
```

$mcs *.cs -out:main.exe

$mono main.exe

50

51

52

53

54

55

56

57

58

59

60

61

62

63

64

The for loop has multiple sections that are usually separated by a semicolon. The first section is labeled as the initializer, used to initialize a variable that acts as a local to the for loop. You cannot access it outside of the loop. Its value can be zero or more than that. The second section of the for loop is a Boolean expression that will be returning true or false. If a particular expression tends to evaluate to true, it will execute the for loop. Otherwise the compiler will execute the loop. The last section is known as an iterator. It defines the decremental or incremental of the for loop variable. The following loop will execute a block of code 30 times. You can increase or decrease the value to increase or decrease the number of repetitions.

```
using System.IO;
using System;
class Program1
{
    static void Main()
    {
        for(int x = 0; x < 30; x++)
{

    Console.WriteLine("The value of x is as follows: {0}", x);
}
    }
}
```

$mcs *.cs -out:main.exe
$mono main.exe
The value of x is as follows: 0
The value of x is as follows: 1
The value of x is as follows: 2

The value of x is as follows: 3
The value of x is as follows: 4
The value of x is as follows: 5
The value of x is as follows: 6
The value of x is as follows: 7
The value of x is as follows: 8
The value of x is as follows: 9
The value of x is as follows: 10
The value of x is as follows: 11
The value of x is as follows: 12
The value of x is as follows: 13
The value of x is as follows: 14
The value of x is as follows: 15
The value of x is as follows: 16
The value of x is as follows: 17
The value of x is as follows: 18
The value of x is as follows: 19
The value of x is as follows: 20
The value of x is as follows: 21
The value of x is as follows: 22
The value of x is as follows: 23
The value of x is as follows: 24
The value of x is as follows: 25
The value of x is as follows: 26
The value of x is as follows: 27
The value of x is as follows: 28
The value of x is as follows: 29

The int x = 0 acts as an initializer. I have defined the int variable x and afterward initialized it with 0. The second section is the expression x < 30. If the condition stands true, the compiler will execute the block of code. When the compiler has executed it, it will move on to the 3rd section that is known as an iterator. The x++ is considered an incremental statement that would increase the value of x by 1. It will check and test the conditional expression at each step and then repeat the code until the conditional expression becomes false. In the next example, I will change the value of the initializer. The loop will execute the code at the point from where the initializer starts. I will change its value from zero to 10.

```
using System.IO;
using System;
class Program1
{
    static void Main()
    {
        for(int x = 10; x < 30; x++)
    {
        Console.WriteLine("The value of x is as follows: {0}", x);
    }
    }
}
```

$mcs *.cs -out:main.exe

$mono main.exe

The value of x is as follows: 10

The value of x is as follows: 11

The value of x is as follows: 12
The value of x is as follows: 13
The value of x is as follows: 14
The value of x is as follows: 15
The value of x is as follows: 16
The value of x is as follows: 17
The value of x is as follows: 18
The value of x is as follows: 19
The value of x is as follows: 20
The value of x is as follows: 21
The value of x is as follows: 22
The value of x is as follows: 23
The value of x is as follows: 24
The value of x is as follows: 25
The value of x is as follows: 26
The value of x is as follows: 27
The value of x is as follows: 28
The value of x is as follows: 29

However, you should make sure that the value of the initializer should not exceed the value of the condition or the compiler will return an empty page.

```
using System.IO;
using System;
class Program1
{
    static void Main()
```

```
        {
            for(int x = 40; x < 30; x++)
    {
        Console.WriteLine("The value of x is as follows: {0}", x);
    }
        }
    }
```
$mcs *.cs -out:main.exe
$mono main.exe

There are some exceptions in regard to the for loop. The initializer, the conditions, and the iterator sections are seen as optional. You can initialize the value even outside of the for loop. After that you can define the condition and the iterator inside the block of code. See the following example.

```
    using System.IO;
    using System;
    class Program1
    {
        static void Main()
        {
            int x = 10;
    for(;;)
    {
        if (x < 30)
        {
```

```
        Console.WriteLine("The value of x is as follows: {0}",
x);
        x++;
    }
    else
        break;
}
    }
}
```

$mcs *.cs -out:main.exe

$mono main.exe

The value of x is as follows: 10

The value of x is as follows: 11

The value of x is as follows: 12

The value of x is as follows: 13

The value of x is as follows: 14

The value of x is as follows: 15

The value of x is as follows: 16

The value of x is as follows: 17

The value of x is as follows: 18

The value of x is as follows: 19

The value of x is as follows: 20

The value of x is as follows: 21

The value of x is as follows: 22

The value of x is as follows: 23

The value of x is as follows: 24

The value of x is as follows: 25

The value of x is as follows: 26

The value of x is as follows: 27

The value of x is as follows: 28

The value of x is as follows: 29

You can see that the results are the same. The for loop gives you the option to fill it in with any kind of numerical data type like decimal, etc.

```
using System.IO;
using System;
class Program1
{
    static void Main()
    {
        for (double d = 1.10D; d < 2.10; d+= 0.01D)
{
    Console.WriteLine("The value of x: {0}", d);
}
    }
}
```

$mcs *.cs -out:main.exe

$mono main.exe

The value of x: 1.1

The value of x: 1.11

The value of x: 1.12

The value of x: 1.13

The value of x: 1.14

The value of x: 1.15

The value of x: 1.16

The value of x: 1.17

The value of x: 1.18

The value of x: 1.19

The value of x: 1.2

The value of x: 1.21

The value of x: 1.22

The value of x: 1.23

The value of x: 1.24

The value of x: 1.25

The value of x: 1.26

The value of x: 1.27

The value of x: 1.28

The value of x: 1.29

The value of x: 1.3

The value of x: 1.31

The value of x: 1.32

The value of x: 1.33

The value of x: 1.34

The value of x: 1.35

The value of x: 1.36

The value of x: 1.37

The value of x: 1.38

The value of x: 1.39

The value of x: 1.4

The value of x: 1.41

The value of x: 1.42

The value of x: 1.43

The value of x: 1.44

The value of x: 1.45

The value of x: 1.46

The value of x: 1.47

The value of x: 1.48

The value of x: 1.49

The value of x: 1.5

The value of x: 1.51

The value of x: 1.52

The value of x: 1.53

The value of x: 1.54

The value of x: 1.55

The value of x: 1.56

The value of x: 1.57

The value of x: 1.58

The value of x: 1.59

The value of x: 1.6

The value of x: 1.61

The value of x: 1.62

The value of x: 1.63

The value of x: 1.64

The value of x: 1.65

The value of x: 1.66

The value of x: 1.67

The value of x: 1.68

The value of x: 1.69

The value of x: 1.7

The value of x: 1.71

The value of x: 1.72

The value of x: 1.73

The value of x: 1.74

The value of x: 1.75

The value of x: 1.76

The value of x: 1.77

The value of x: 1.78

The value of x: 1.79

The value of x: 1.8

The value of x: 1.81

The value of x: 1.82

The value of x: 1.83

The value of x: 1.84

The value of x: 1.85

The value of x: 1.86

The value of x: 1.87

The value of x: 1.88

The value of x: 1.89

The value of x: 1.9

The value of x: 1.91

The value of x: 1.92

The value of x: 1.93

The value of x: 1.94

The value of x: 1.95

The value of x: 1.96

The value of x: 1.97

The value of x: 1.98

The value of x: 1.99

The value of x: 2

The value of x: 2.01

The value of x: 2.02

The value of x: 2.03

The value of x: 2.04

The value of x: 2.05

The value of x: 2.06

The value of x: 2.07

The value of x: 2.08

The value of x: 2.09

The value of x: 2.1

Up until now you have seen how you can increment the value in the code with a for loop. You also have the option to decrease the value of the variable by using the following code.

```
using System.IO;
using System;
class Program1
{
    static void Main()
    {
        for(int x = 10; x > 0; x--)
    {
        Console.WriteLine("The value of x is: {0}", x);
    }
        }
}
```

$mcs *.cs -out:main.exe

$mono main.exe

The value of x is: 10

The value of x is: 9

The value of x is: 8

The value of x is: 7

The value of x is: 6

The value of x is: 5

The value of x is: 4

The value of x is: 3

The value of x is: 2

The value of x is: 1

You also can push the figure into negatives by setting conditions that way. This can be handy when you move on to building programs in C#. Some programs demand negative numbers, calculated by a loop.

```
using System.IO;
using System;
class Program1
{
    static void Main()
    {
        for(int x = 10; x > -10; x--)
{
    Console.WriteLine("The value of x is: {0}", x);
}
```

```
        }
}
```

$mcs *.cs -out:main.exe

$mono main.exe

The value of x is: 10

The value of x is: 9

The value of x is: 8

The value of x is: 7

The value of x is: 6

The value of x is: 5

The value of x is: 4

The value of x is: 3

The value of x is: 2

The value of x is: 1

The value of x is: 0

The value of x is: -1

The value of x is: -2

The value of x is: -3

The value of x is: -4

The value of x is: -5

The value of x is: -6

The value of x is: -7

The value of x is: -8

The value of x is: -9

Even if you have a condition, set at the higher number, you can exit the loop at will by using the break keyword. I will take a previous example and enter in it the break keyword to see how it stops the loop and allows you to exit the loop at will.

```
using System.IO;
using System;
class Program1
{
    static void Main()
    {
        for (int x = 0; x < 14; x++)
{
    if( x == 7 )
        break;
    Console.WriteLine("The Value of x is: {0}", x);
}
    }
}
```

$mcs *.cs -out:main.exe
$mono main.exe
The value of x is: 0
The value of x is: 1
The value of x is: 2
The value of x is: 3
The value of x is: 4
The value of x is: 5
The value of x is: 6

Even though the condition was set to loop through the block of code until it reached the figure 14, the loop stopped at 7.

Multiple Expressions

A for loop will also include multiple iterators and initializer statements that are usually separated by a comma, as is shown below.

```
using System.IO;
using System;
class Program1
{
    static void Main()
    {
        for (int x = 0, y = 0; x+y < 15; x++, y++)
    {
        Console.WriteLine("Value of x: {0}, Value of y: {1} ",
    x,y);
    }
    }
}
```

$mcs *.cs -out:main.exe
$mono main.exe
Value of x: 0, Value of y: 0
Value of x: 1, Value of y: 1
Value of x: 2, Value of y: 2
Value of x: 3, Value of y: 3
Value of x: 4, Value of y: 4

Value of x: 5, Value of y: 5

Value of x: 6, Value of y: 6

Value of x: 7, Value of y: 7

You also can add an iterator and an initializer in the *for* loop. This is a more complex but smart form of writing a for loop in C#.

```
using System.IO;
using System;
class Program
{
    static void Main()
    {
        int x = 0, y = 10;
for (Console.WriteLine($"Initializer: x={x}, y={y}");
    x++ < y--;
    Console.WriteLine($"Iterator: x={x}, y={y}"))
    {
    }
    }
}
$mcs *.cs -out:main.exe
$mono main.exe
Initializer: x=0, y=10
Iterator: x=1, y=9
Iterator: x=2, y=8
Iterator: x=3, y=7
Iterator: x=4, y=6
Iterator: x=5, y=5
```

C# Nested For Loop

You can nest a for loop inside of another for loop. The function is the same as with the while loop. There is iteration. One loop simply runs like a normal loop while the other runs through each value of the second loop.

```
using System.IO;
using System;
class Program1
{
    static void Main()
    {
        for (int x = 0; x < 10; x++)
{
    for(int y =x; y < 6; y++)
        Console.WriteLine("The value of x is: {0}, The value of
Y is: {1} ", x,y);
    }
    }
}
```

$mcs *.cs -out:main.exe
$mono main.exe
The value of x is: 0, The value of Y is: 0
The value of x is: 0, The value of Y is: 1
The value of x is: 0, The value of Y is: 2
The value of x is: 0, The value of Y is: 3
The value of x is: 0, The value of Y is: 4
The value of x is: 0, The value of Y is: 5

The value of x is: 1, The value of Y is: 1

The value of x is: 1, The value of Y is: 2

The value of x is: 1, The value of Y is: 3

The value of x is: 1, The value of Y is: 4

The value of x is: 1, The value of Y is: 5

The value of x is: 2, The value of Y is: 2

The value of x is: 2, The value of Y is: 3

The value of x is: 2, The value of Y is: 4

The value of x is: 2, The value of Y is: 5

The value of x is: 3, The value of Y is: 3

The value of x is: 3, The value of Y is: 4

The value of x is: 3, The value of Y is: 5

The value of x is: 4, The value of Y is: 4

The value of x is: 4, The value of Y is: 5

The value of x is: 5, The value of Y is: 5

The C# Foreach Loop

There is another loop known as the foreach loop, which is exclusively used for looping through an array. We had created an array of fruits in the previous chapters. I will take the same array and integrate it in a foreach loop. The block of code will output all the elements in the fruits array by deploying a foreach loop.

```
using System.IO;
using System;
class Program1
{
    static void Main()
```

```
        {
        string[] fruits = {"guava", "grapefruit", "apple", "banana",
"strawberry", "blueberry", "jackfruit", "dragonfruit", "peach",
"apricot"};
        foreach (string x in fruits)
    {
      Console.WriteLine(x);
    }
        }
}
```

$mcs *.cs -out:main.exe

$mono main.exe

guava

grapefruit

apple

banana

strawberry

blueberry

jackfruit

dragonfruit

peach

apricot

See how the for loop iterates through all items of an array. If you include in the code the length property, you can fix how many times you want the for loop to iterate through the items inside the array.

using System.IO;

```csharp
using System;
class Program1
{
    static void Main()
    {
        string[] fruits = {"guava", "grapefruit", "apple", "banana",
"strawberry", "blueberry", "jackfruit", "dragonfruit", "peach",
"apricot"};
        for (int x = 0; x < fruits.Length; x++)
{
  Console.WriteLine(fruits[x]);
}
    }
}
```
$mcs *.cs -out:main.exe
$mono main.exe
guava
grapefruit
apple
banana
strawberry
blueberry
jackfruit
dragonfruit
peach
apricot

You can initialize the loop at a later point by changing the value of the initializer. Take a look at the following example.

```
using System.IO;
using System;
class Program1
{
    static void Main()
    {
        string[] fruits = {"guava", "grapefruit", "apple", "banana",
"strawberry", "blueberry", "jackfruit", "dragonfruit", "peach",
"apricot"};
        for (int x = 2; x < fruits.Length; x++)
{
    Console.WriteLine(fruits[x]);
}
    }
}
$mcs *.cs -out:main.exe
$mono main.exe
apple
banana
strawberry
blueberry
jackfruit
dragonfruit
peach
apricot
```

C# Foreach Loop for Sorting Arrays

There are a big number of array methods available such as Sort(). This specific method sorts out the array in alphabetical order or ascending order. You can use this special function if you are creating a game in C#. Take the array of fruits. If your game has a vendor who sells fruits, you can put the array in alphabetical order if a buyer asks about the types of fruits the vendor has. The player will be able to display the list or speak through the vendor in the alphabetical order or the ascending order. I will use both techniques in this section. The sorting function through the foreach loop makes your games and program clean and interesting at the same time.

```
using System.IO;
using System;
class Program1
{
    static void Main()
    {
        string[] fruits = {"guava", "grapefruit", "apple", "banana",
"strawberry", "blueberry", "jackfruit", "dragonfruit", "peach",
"apricot"};
        Array.Sort(fruits);
foreach (string x in fruits)
{
  Console.WriteLine(x);
}
    }
}
```

apple

apricot

banana

blueberry

dragonfruit

grapefruit

guava

jackfruit

peach

strawberry

For sorting an array in the ascending order, I will use an array of integers.

```
using System.IO;
using System;
class Program1
{
    static void Main()
    {
    int[] myNum = {5, 2, 1, 3, 8, 7, 9};
Array.Sort(myNum);
foreach (int x in myNum)
{
  Console.WriteLine(x);
}
```

```
        }
    }
```

$mcs *.cs -out:main.exe

$mono main.exe

```
1
2
3
5
7
8
9
```

C# Break and Continue Statements

I have already used the break statement in the previous chapters. I paired it up with the switch statement. You also can use the break statement to move out of a loop.

```
using System.IO;
using System;
class Program1
{
    static void Main()
    {
        for (int x = 0; x < 10; x++)
    {
      if (x == 6)
      {
        break;
```

```
        }
    Console.WriteLine(x);
    }
        }
}
```
$mcs *.cs -out:main.exe
$mono main.exe
0
1
2
3
4
5

The next is the continue statement. It breaks an iteration once at the location you specify, and then continue with the next iteration in the loop.

```
using System.IO;
using System;
class Program1
{
    static void Main()
    {
        for (int x = 0; x < 15; x++)
{
  if (x == 6)
    {
```

```
    continue;
  }
  Console.WriteLine(x);
}
}
}
```
$mcs *.cs -out:main.exe
$mono main.exe
0
1
2
3
4
5
7
8
9
10
11
12
13
14

You can see that the loop skipped the number 6 as I had specified for not being iterated. You also can use the break and continue statements in a similar fashion in the while loop. See the following example of the break statement.

```
using System.IO;
using System;
class Program1
{
    static void Main()
    {
        int x = 0;
while (x < 15)
{
  Console.WriteLine(x);
  x++;
  if (x ==6)
  {
   break;
  }
}
}
}
```

$mcs *.cs -out:main.exe
$mono main.exe
0
1
2
3
4
5

In the next example, I will use the continue statement.

```csharp
using System.IO;
using System;
class Program1
{
    static void Main()
    {
        int x = 0;
while (x < 20)
{
  if (x == 10)
  {
    x++;
    continue;
  }
  Console.WriteLine(x);
  x++;
}
}
}
```

$mcs *.cs -out:main.exe
$mono main.exe
0
1
2
3
4
5
6

Chapter Six

C# Methods

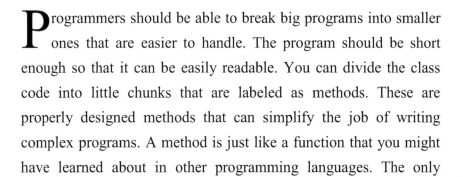

Programmers should be able to break big programs into smaller ones that are easier to handle. The program should be short enough so that it can be easily readable. You can divide the class code into little chunks that are labeled as methods. These are properly designed methods that can simplify the job of writing complex programs. A method is just like a function that you might have learned about in other programming languages. The only difference is that a method is part of a C# class.

Methods are statements that allow a programmer to reuse an already written block of code. It saves excessive use of memory and eases off the coding process. Methods also increase the readability of code. In simple words, a method is also known as a collection of statements that perform particular tasks and likewise return the results. There may come certain methods along your way which don't return anything.

Defining Methods

A method is generally defined with a name that is followed by a parenthesis. There also are some predefined methods in C# such as the Main() which you have been acquainted with right from the start of the book.

```
using System.IO;
using System;
class Program1
{
    static void ThisMethod()
    {
      Console.WriteLine("Let's execute it!");
    }
    static void Main(string[] args)
    {
      ThisMethod();
    }
}
$mcs *.cs -out:main.exe
$mono main.exe
Let's execute it!
```

I have created a method, assign it a string value, and then called it in the end. In the above block of code, the keyword static means that this method belongs to the Program1 class. The keyword void means that the method doesn't have a return value. You can call a method as many times as you need to.

```
using System.IO;
using System;
class Program1
{
    static void ThisMethod()
    {
     Console.WriteLine("Let's execute it!");
    }
    static void Main(string[] args)
    {
     ThisMethod();
        ThisMethod();
          ThisMethod();
            ThisMethod();
    }
}
$mcs *.cs -out:main.exe
$mono main.exe
Let's execute it!
Let's execute it!
Let's execute it!
Let's execute it!
```

Parameters

You can pass on information to a method by using parameters. These parameters tend to act as variables within the method. They are specified after the name of the method inside of the parameters.

Add many parameters as you want in your program. Separate them with a comma.

```
using System.IO;
using System;

namespace MyApp
{
class Program1
{
    static void ThisMethod(string fname)
    {
    Console.WriteLine(fname + " will come to the class after playing football");
}
static void Main(string[] args)
{
  ThisMethod("Jack");
  ThisMethod("Tom");
  ThisMethod("Fin");
  ThisMethod("Jasmine");
  ThisMethod("Sylvia");
}
    }
    }
```
$mcs *.cs -out:main.exe
$mono main.exe
Jack will come to the class after playing football

Tom will come to the class after playing football

Fin will come to the class after playing football

Jasmine will come to the class after playing football

Sylvia will come to the class after playing football

You also can add default parameters to the methods so that if you left them empty, it is filled by the default parameters.

```
using System.IO;
using System;

namespace MyApp
{
class Program1
{
    static void ThisMethod(string fname = " Donald will come
to the class after playing football")
    {
    Console.WriteLine(fname);
}
static void Main(string[] args)
{
  ThisMethod();
  ThisMethod();
  ThisMethod();
}
  }
  }
```

```
$mcs *.cs -out:main.exe
$mono main.exe
```

Donald will come to the class after playing football

Donald will come to the class after playing football

Donald will come to the class after playing football

Multiple Parameters

You can pass on more than one parameter to the method if you are building a complex program.

```
using System.IO;
using System;

namespace MyApp
{
class Program1
{
    static void ThisMethod(string fname, int yearofbirth)
    {
    Console.WriteLine(fname + " was born in " + yearofbirth);
}
static void Main(string[] args)
{
  ThisMethod("Jack", 2000);
  ThisMethod("Tom", 1998);
  ThisMethod("Sylvia", 1995);
  ThisMethod("Yik", 1992);
}
```

```
      }
   }
```

$mcs *.cs -out:main.exe
$mono main.exe

Jack was born in 2000

Tom was born in 1998

Sylvia was born in 1995

Yik was born in 1992

Return Values

You can use the void keyword if you want the method to return a value. This technique can be used in programs that involve mathematical calculations. See the following examples.

```csharp
using System.IO;
using System;

namespace MyApp
{
class Program1
{
   static int ThisMethod(int y)
    {
  return 10 + y;
}
static void Main(string[] args)
{
  Console.WriteLine(ThisMethod(3));
```

```
}
    }
    }
```

$mcs *.cs -out:main.exe
$mono main.exe

13

I will now change the values and use a different mathematical operator to see the result.

```
using System.IO;
using System;

namespace MyApp
{
class Program1
{
    static int ThisMethod(int y)
    {
  return 15 - y;
}
static void Main(string[] args)
{
  Console.WriteLine(ThisMethod(50));
}
    }
    }
```

$mcs *.cs -out:main.exe
$mono main.exe

-35

You can use the operator for the multiplication of two digits.

```csharp
using System.IO;
using System;

namespace MyApp
{
class Program1
{
    static int ThisMethod(int y)
    {
  return 15 * y;
}
static void Main(string[] args)
{
  Console.WriteLine(ThisMethod(50));
}
    }
    }
```

$mcs *.cs -out:main.exe
$mono main.exe
750

This last operator for the division.

```csharp
using System.IO;
using System;

namespace MyApp
{
class Program1
```

```
{
    static int ThisMethod(int y)
    {
    return 15 / y;
}
static void Main(string[] args)
{
    Console.WriteLine(ThisMethod(50));
}
    }
    }
```

$mcs *.cs -out:main.exe
$mono main.exe
0

Two Parameters

Now I will be using two parameters in the same method.

```
using System.IO;
using System;

namespace MyApp
{
class Program1
{
    static int ThisMethod(int y, int z)
    {
    return y + z;
```

159

```
}
static void Main(string[] args)
{
  Console.WriteLine(ThisMethod(5, 6));
}
    }
    }
```

$mcs *.cs -out:main.exe
$mono main.exe
11
I will add more console statements to apply the method to different parameters.

```
using System.IO;
using System;

namespace MyApp
{
class Program1
{
    static int ThisMethod(int y, int z)
    {
  return y - z;
}
static void Main(string[] args)
{
  Console.WriteLine(ThisMethod(15, 6));
  Console.WriteLine(ThisMethod(355, 6));
    Console.WriteLine(ThisMethod(35, 6));
```

```
}
    }
    }
```

$mcs *.cs -out:main.exe
$mono main.exe

9

349

29

You can apply different mathematical operators to get the desired results. See the following block of code.

```
using System.IO;
using System;

namespace MyApp
{
class Program1
{
    static int ThisMethod(int y, int z)
    {
    return y * z;
}
static void Main(string[] args)
{
  Console.WriteLine(ThisMethod(15, 6));
  Console.WriteLine(ThisMethod(355, 6));
    Console.WriteLine(ThisMethod(35, 6));
}
    }
```

```
    }
```

90

2130

210

Here comes division.

```csharp
using System.IO;
using System;

namespace MyApp
{
class Program1
{
    static int ThisMethod(int y, int z)
    {
  return y / z;
}
static void Main(string[] args)
{
  Console.WriteLine(ThisMethod(15, 6));
  Console.WriteLine(ThisMethod(355, 6));
    Console.WriteLine(ThisMethod(35, 6));
}
    }
    }
```

2

59

5

Store Result

You have the option to store the result in a variable. Suppose you are creating a program in which you invite users to fill in their input which you can view later on. You can direct the input to a variable so that it would be easier to access whenever you need to view it.

```csharp
using System.IO;
using System;

namespace MyApp
{
class Program1
{
    static int ThisMethod(int y, int z)
    {
  return y / z;
}
static void Main(string[] args)
{

  int x = ThisMethod(35 , 6);
    Console.WriteLine(x);
}
  }
```

```
    }
$mcs *.cs -out:main.exe
$mono main.exe
5
```

Chapter Seven

Object-Oriented Programming

This chapter will walk you through the ins and outs of object-oriented programming. C# supports object-oriented programming. A class in C# is a bundle of data and functions that belong together into a single tidy package. C# gives you the freedom to create classes and build programs. These are basic concepts of OOP. You can model real-life objects on classes. A class is like a user-defined blueprint from which you can create objects. A class, generally, combines methods and fields into a single unit. Classes in C# support polymorphism.

A class contains a single keyword namely class, followed by an identifier, and each class may have many different attributes. An object is a basic unit of object-oriented programming, and may reflect any real-life entity. You can create many objects through C# programs. Many objects tend to interact by invoking different methods. A particular object consists of a state which is represented by different attributes of a particular object. It also reflects the properties of the object. Another feature of the object is its behavior which is represented by different methods of a particular object. It also reflects how an object responds. The third feature of a class is identity, which gives a unique name to a particular object, and also enables it to interact with different other objects present in the same class.

For example, a cat is an object. It rolls on the ground, sits and jumps. When we create an object in a class, the class will be instantiated. All the different instances tend to share different attributes and behavior of a class. There may be more than one instance in a class.

Creating C# Class

I will be using a new operator to initialize an object in a class.

using System;

// Declaration of class

```java
public class Cat {

    // Instance Variables
    String cname;
    String cbreed;
    int cage;
    String ccolor;

    public Cat(String cname, String cbreed,
            int cage, String ccolor)
    {
        this.cname = cname;
        this.cbreed = cbreed;
        this.cage = cage;
        this.ccolor = ccolor;
    }

    // This is Property 1
    public String getName()
    {
        return cname;
    }

    // This is Property 2
    public String getBreed()
    {
        return cbreed;
    }
```

```java
// This is Property 3
public int getAge()
{
    return cage;
}


// This is Property 4
public String getColor()
{
    return ccolor;
}


// Method 1
public String toString()
{
    return ("Hi this is " + this.getName()
        + ".\nYou will be pleased to know that my breed,
age and color are " + this.getBreed()
        + ", " + this.getAge() + ", " + this.getColor());
}

// This is the Main Method
public static void Main(String[] args)
    {

        // Mow I am Creating an object
        Cat timmy = new Cat("Timmy", "ragdoll",6, "black.");
```

```
        Console.WriteLine(timmy.toString());
    }
}
```

$mcs *.cs -out:main.exe
$mono main.exe
Hi this is Timmy.

You will be pleased to know that my breed, age and color are ragdoll, 6, black.

You can add as many instances to a single as you like. The one instance is timmy. Now I will add more instances to the same class.

```
using System;

// Declaration of class
public class Cat {

    // Instance Variables
    String cname;
    String cbreed;
    int cage;
    String ccolor;


    public Cat(String cname, String cbreed,
            int cage, String ccolor)
    {
        this.cname = cname;
```

```java
        this.cbreed = cbreed;
        this.cage = cage;
        this.ccolor = ccolor;
    }

    // This is Property 1
    public String getName()
    {
        return cname;
    }

    // This is Property 2
    public String getBreed()
    {
        return cbreed;
    }

    // This is Property 3
    public int getAge()
    {
        return cage;
    }

    // This is Property 4
    public String getColor()
    {
        return ccolor;
    }
```

```csharp
// Method 1
public String toString()
{
    return ("Hi this is " + this.getName()
        + ".\nYou will be pleased to know that my breed,
age and color are as followed : " + this.getBreed()
        + ", " + this.getAge() + ", " + this.getColor());
}

// This is the Main Method
public static void Main(String[] args)
{

    // Mow I am Creating an object
    Cat timmy = new Cat("Timmy", "ragdoll", 6 , "black.");
    Console.WriteLine(timmy.toString()) ;

    Cat tim = new Cat("Tim", "ragdoll", 9 , "white.");
    Console.WriteLine(tim.toString()) ;

    Cat hitman = new Cat("Hitman", "Savannah", 9 ,
"brown.");
    Console.WriteLine(hitman.toString()) ;

    Cat beamer = new Cat("Beamer", "sphynx", 8, "white.");
    Console.WriteLine(beamer.toString()) ;
}
```

```
}
```

$mcs *.cs -out:main.exe
$mono main.exe
Hi this is Timmy.

You will be pleased to know that my breed, age and color are as followed : ragdoll, 6, black.

Hi this is Tim.

You will be pleased to know that my breed, age and color are as followed : ragdoll, 9, white.

Hi this is Hitman.

You will be pleased to know that my breed, age and color are as followed : Savannah, 9, brown.

Hi this is Beamer.

You will be pleased to know that my breed, age and color are as followed : sphynx, 8, white.

You can see that I have created four different objects through the process of instantiation. You can add as many instances to the cat class as you like. This class has a single constructor.

The Car Class

I will model a car using the same instances.

```csharp
using System;

// Declaration of class
public class Car {

    // Instance Variables
    String cname;
    String cmodel;
    int cmake;
    String ccolor;


    public Car(String cname, String cmodel,
            int cmake, String ccolor)
    {
        this.cname = cname;
        this.cmodel = cmodel;
        this.cmake = cmake;
        this.ccolor = ccolor;
    }

    // This is Property 1
    public String getName()
    {
        return cname;
```

```java
}

// This is Property 2
public String getModel()
{
    return cmodel;
}

// This is Property 3
public int getMake()
{
    return cmake;
}

// This is Property 4
public String getColor()
{
    return ccolor;
}

// Method 1
public String toString()
{
    return ("This car is " + this.getName()
        + ".\nIts model, year and color are as followed
respectively : " + this.getModel()
        + ", " + this.getMake() + ", " + this.getColor());
}
```

```csharp
// This is the Main Method
public static void Main(String[] args)
    {

        // Mow I am creating an object
        Car bmw = new Car("BMW", "X1", 2008 , "black.");
        Console.WriteLine(bmw.toString()) ;



    }

}
```

$mcs *.cs -out:main.exe
$mono main.exe
This car is BMW.

Its model, year and color are as followed respectively : X1, 2008, black.

Now I will add three more cars to the same class. You don't have to change anything in the class. All you are required to do is make the necessary changes in the instances that I have added. Fill it in with the details by which you want to create more objects.

```csharp
using System;


// Declaration of class
```

```java
public class Car {

    // Instance Variables
    String cname;
    String cmodel;
    int cmake;
    String ccolor;


    public Car(String cname, String cmodel,
               int cmake, String ccolor)
    {
        this.cname = cname;
        this.cmodel = cmodel;
        this.cmake = cmake;
        this.ccolor = ccolor;
    }

    // This is Property 1
    public String getName()
    {
        return cname;
    }

    // This is Property 2
    public String getModel()
    {
        return cmodel;
```

```
    }

    // This is Property 3
    public int getMake()
    {
        return cmake;
    }

    // This is Property 4
    public String getColor()
    {
        return ccolor;
    }

    // Method 1
    public String toString()
    {
        return ("This car is known as " + this.getName()
            + ".\nIts model, year and color are as followed
respectively : " + this.getModel()
            + ", " + this.getMake() + ", " + this.getColor());
    }

// This is the Main Method
public static void Main(String[] args)
    {

        // Mow I am Creating an object
```

```
Car bmw = new Car("BMW", "X1", 2008 , "black.");
Console.WriteLine(bmw.toString()) ;

Car rangerover = new Car("Range Rover", "Velar", 2016
, "black.");
Console.WriteLine(rangerover.toString()) ;

Car audi = new Car("Audi", "A4 Sedan", 2014 ,
"black.");
Console.WriteLine(audi.toString()) ;

Car mercedes = new Car("Mercedes", "C-Class", 2019 ,
"white.");
Console.WriteLine(mercedes.toString()) ;

}


}
```

$mcs *.cs -out:main.exe
$mono main.exe
This car is known as BMW.

Its model, year and color are as followed respectively : X1, 2008, black.

This car is known as Range Rover.

Its model, year and color are as followed respectively : Velar, 2016, black.

This car is known as Audi.

Its model, year and color are as followed respectively : A4 Sedan, 2014, black.

This car is known as Mercedes.

Its model, year and color are as followed respectively : C-Class, 2019, white.

Class Members

In the following I will once again create a car class which will have two fields, one for the color and the other for the speed.

```
using System;
namespace MyApp

{
  class Cars
  {
    string ccolor = "white";
    int cmaxSpeed = 150;
    static void Main(string[] args)
    {
      Cars myObject = new Cars();
      Console.WriteLine(myObject.ccolor);
      Console.WriteLine(myObject.cmaxSpeed);
    }
  }
```

}
$mcs *.cs -out:main.exe
$mono main.exe
white
150

If you want to let your users fill in the fields of the objects, you can fill them later on while you are creating class objects.

```
using System;
namespace MyApp

{
  class Cars
  {
    string ccolor ;
    int cmaxSpeed ;
    static void Main(string[] args)
    {
      Cars myObject = new Cars();
      myObject.ccolor = "white";
      myObject.cmaxSpeed = 150;
      Console.WriteLine(myObject.ccolor);
      Console.WriteLine(myObject.cmaxSpeed);
    }
  }
}
```
$mcs *.cs -out:main.exe

white
150

I am now going to add two more fields to the same class to show how easy it is to add fields to a single class.

```
using System;
namespace MyApp

{
  class Cars
  {
    string ccolor ;
    int cmaxSpeed ;
    int cmake ;
    string cmodel;
    static void Main (string[] args)
    {
      Cars myObject = new Cars();
       myObject.ccolor = "white";
      myObject.cmaxSpeed = 150;
      myObject.cmake = 2002;
      myObject.cmodel = "BMW";
      Console.WriteLine (myObject.ccolor) ;
      Console.WriteLine (myObject.cmaxSpeed) ;
      Console.WriteLine (myObject.cmake) ;
      Console.WriteLine (myObject.cmodel) ;
```

```
    }
   }
  }
```

$mcs *.cs -out:main.exe

$mono main.exe

white

150

2002

BMW

You have already learned about how you can add different objects to a single class. There is another method that you can use to create objects.

```
using System;
namespace MyApp

{
  class Cars
  {
    string ccolor ;
    int cmaxSpeed ;
    int cmake ;
    string cmodel;
    static void Main (string[] args)
    {
      Cars BMW = new Cars();
      BMW.ccolor = "Black" ;
```

```
BMW.cmaxSpeed = 200 ;
BMW.cmake = 2015 ;
BMW.cmodel = "Turismo" ;

Cars Audi = new Cars();
Audi.ccolor = "Black" ;
Audi.cmaxSpeed = 250 ;
Audi.cmake = 2019 ;
Audi.cmodel = "A4" ;

Cars Mercedes = new Cars();
Mercedes.ccolor = "Silver" ;
Mercedes.cmaxSpeed = 100 ;
Mercedes.cmake = 2013 ;
Mercedes.cmodel = "C-Class" ;


Console.WriteLine (BMW.ccolor) ;
Console.WriteLine (BMW.cmaxSpeed) ;
Console.WriteLine (BMW.cmake) ;
Console.WriteLine (BMW.cmodel) ;

Console.WriteLine (Audi.ccolor) ;
Console.WriteLine (Audi.cmaxSpeed) ;
Console.WriteLine (Audi.cmake) ;
Console.WriteLine (Audi.cmodel) ;

Console.WriteLine (Mercedes.ccolor) ;
```

```
    Console.WriteLine (Mercedes.cmaxSpeed) ;
    Console.WriteLine (Mercedes.cmake) ;
    Console.WriteLine (Mercedes.cmodel) ;
  }
 }
}
```
$mcs *.cs -out:main.exe
$mono main.exe
Black
200
2015
Turismo
Black
250
2019
A4
Silver
100
2013
C-Class

Class Methods

Methods are inherent to classes and they are used to define how an object inside of a class behaves. Just like the fields, you have the power to access different methods by using the dot syntax. You must note that methods should be public. You must remember that you use the method name along with the pair of parentheses and a semicolon. I will add a method to the cars class mentioned above.

```csharp
using System;
namespace MyApp

{
  class Cars
  {
    string ccolor ;
    int cmaxSpeed ;
    int cmake ;
    string cmodel;

    public void fullThrot()    // method
    {
      Console.WriteLine("These cars go from zero to hundred in five seconds! ");
    }
    static void Main (string[] args)
    {

      Cars BMW = new Cars();
      BMW.ccolor = "Black" ;
      BMW.cmaxSpeed = 210 ;
      BMW.cmake = 2013 ;
      BMW.cmodel = "A4" ;

      Cars Audi = new Cars();
      Audi.ccolor = "Black" ;
      Audi.cmaxSpeed = 250 ;
```

```
Audi.cmake = 2019 ;
Audi.cmodel = "A4" ;

Cars Mercedes = new Cars();
Mercedes.ccolor = "Silver" ;
Mercedes.cmaxSpeed = 100 ;
Mercedes.cmake = 2013 ;
Mercedes.cmodel = "C-Class" ;

Cars myObj = new Cars();

myObj.fullThrot();

Console.WriteLine (BMW.ccolor) ;
Console.WriteLine (BMW.cmaxSpeed) ;
Console.WriteLine (BMW.cmake) ;
Console.WriteLine (BMW.cmodel) ;

Console.WriteLine (Audi.ccolor) ;
Console.WriteLine (Audi.cmaxSpeed) ;
Console.WriteLine (Audi.cmake) ;
Console.WriteLine (Audi.cmodel) ;

Console.WriteLine (Mercedes.ccolor) ;
Console.WriteLine (Mercedes.cmaxSpeed) ;
Console.WriteLine (Mercedes.cmake) ;
Console.WriteLine (Mercedes.cmodel) ;
}
```

}

}

$mcs *.cs -out:main.exe

$mono main.exe

These cars go from zero to a hundred in five seconds!

Black

210

2013

A4

Black

250

2019

A4

Silver

100

2013

C-Class

In the above example, the method was applied to all the instances that I had created. You can add more instances to the class and also create and add more methods as well to experiment how far you can go with the programming. It would really be fun and interesting.

You can create multiple classes to organize the program in a better and efficient way. For example, you can create a separate class for field methods and another one for the execution.

C# Class Constructor

This is a special method that you can use to initialize objects. Its advantage is that it can be called when a class object is created. You can use it to settle down the initial values for different fields.

```
using System;
namespace MyApp
{
  // this will create a Car class
  class Cars
  {
    public string cmodel;  // This will create a field
    // I will now Create the class constructor for the above-
mentioned Cars class
    public Cars()
    {
      cmodel = "C-classic"; // This will set initial value for the
model
    }
    static void Main(string[] args)
    {
      Cars Ford = new Cars();
      Console.WriteLine(Ford.cmodel);
    }
  }
}
$mcs *.cs -out:main.exe
$mono main.exe
```

C-classic

Try it with another model.

```
using System;
namespace MyApp
{
  // this will create a Car class
  class Cars
  {
    public string cmodel;  // This will create a field
     public string ccolor;
      public int cmake;
    // I will now Create the class constructor for the above
mentioned Cars class
    public Cars()
     {
       cmodel = "C-classic"; // This will set initial value for the
model
       ccolor = "White";
       cmake = 2002;


     }
    static void Main(string[] args)
     {
      Cars Ford = new Cars();
      Console.WriteLine(Ford.cmodel);
      Console.WriteLine(Ford.ccolor);
      Console.WriteLine(Ford.cmake);
```

```
      Cars BMW = new Cars();
      Console.WriteLine(BMW.cmodel);
      Console.WriteLine(BMW.ccolor);
      Console.WriteLine(BMW.cmake);
    }
   }
}
```

$mcs *.cs -out:main.exe
$mono main.exe
C-classic
White
2002
C-classic
White
2002

The name of the constructor must match the name of the class. Also, there should not any return type such as int or void. You can call the constructor when the object is created. All classes possess constructors by default. If you don't create one yourself, C# will do that for you.

You can pass on parameters to a constructor just like methods. See the following example.

```
using System;
namespace MyApp
{
```

```
class Cars
{
  public string cmodel;

  public Cars (string cmodelName)
  {
    cmodel = cmodelName;
  }
  static void Main(string[] args)
  {
    Cars Ford = new Cars("Mustang");
    Console.WriteLine(Ford.cmodel);
  }
 }
}
```

$mcs *.cs -out:main.exe
$mono main.exe
Mustang

Multiple Parameters

You can add to the class as many parameters as you want to.

```
using System;
namespace MyApp
{
// this will create a Car class
class Cars
{
```

191

```csharp
public string cmodel;  // This will create a field
public string ccolor;
public int cmake;
// I will now Create the class constructor for the above
mentioned Cars class
public Cars(string modelName, string modelColor, int
modelMake)
{
cmodel = modelName ; // This will set initial value for the
model
ccolor = modelColor ;
cmake = modelMake ;

}
static void Main(string[] args)
{
Cars Ford = new Cars("Mustang", "White", 2009);
Console.WriteLine(Ford.ccolor + " " + Ford.cmake + " " +
Ford.cmodel);

Cars BMW = new Cars("BMW", "White", 2009);
Console.WriteLine(BMW.ccolor + " " + BMW.cmake + "
" + BMW.cmodel);

Cars Merc = new Cars("Mercedes", "Black", 2010);
Console.WriteLine(Merc.ccolor + " " + Merc.cmake + " "
+ Merc.cmodel);
```

```
        Cars Rangerover = new Cars("Rangerover", "Black",
    2015);
        Console.WriteLine(Rangerover.ccolor + " " +
    Rangerover.cmake + " " + Rangerover.cmodel);


    }
    }
}
```

$mcs *.cs -out:main.exe
$mono main.exe
White 2009 Mustang
White 2009 BMW
Black 2010 Mercedes
Black 2015 Rangerover

C# Properties

Combined with the properties is the concept of encapsulation. Encapsulation means that sensitive data ought to be hidden from outside users. You can do this by declaring variables and fields as private. You also can do that by providing public, set and get methods through properties to update and access the value of a particular private field.

You only can access private variables inside the same class. No outside class can access it. However, it can be done through properties. A property can be defined as a combination of a method and a variable. There generally are two methods of property; one is the get and the other is the set method.

```
using System;
namespace MyApp
{
  class Cars
  {
  private string cname; // field
  public string cName   // property
   {
    get { return cname; }
    set { cname = value; }
   }
}
class Program1
{
  static void Main(string[] args)
   {
   Cars thisObj = new Cars();
   thisObj.cName = "BMW";
   Console.WriteLine(thisObj.cName);
   }
 }
}
$mcs *.cs -out:main.exe
$mono main.exe
BMW
```

We can change the object in the class with the same properties. See the following example.

```
using System;
namespace MyApp
{
 class Cars
{
 private string cname; // field
 public string cName  // property
 {
  get { return cname; }
  set { cname = value; }
 }
}
class Program1
{
 static void Main(string[] args)
 {
  Cars thisObj = new Cars();
  thisObj.cName = "Mercedes";
  Console.WriteLine(thisObj.cName);
 }
}
}
$mcs *.cs -out:main.exe
$mono main.exe
Mercedes
```

There is another way to write properties in a class. C# offers shorthand to automatically write properties if you don't want to define the field for the property. All you are required to write is set; and get; within the scope of the property. In the following example, I will write the properties automatically through shorthand. The difference between the two methods is that you have to write less code that way.

```
using System;
namespace MyApp
{
  class Cars
{
  public string cName  // property
  { get; set; }
}
class Program1
{
  static void Main(string[] args)
  {
   Cars thisObj = new Cars();
   thisObj.cName = "Mercedes";
   Console.WriteLine(thisObj.cName);
  }
 }
 }
$mcs *.cs -out:main.exe
$mono main.exe
Mercedes
```

Chapter Eight

C# Classes Explained Further

In C# you can inherit methods and fields from one class to another one. The concept of inheritance concept is generally divided into two categories. One is named the Base Class which is the class from which the other class is inherited. The other one is the Derived Class which inherits properties from the parent class. To start the process of inheritance, you can use the : symbol. In the following example, I will create one parent and one child class to show how you can use them in real programming.

```
using System;
namespace MyApp
{
  class Cars  // base class (the parent class)
{
  public string company = "Ford";  // The Cars field
  public void honk()          // The Cars method
  {
    Console.WriteLine("This is a brand new: ");
  }
}
```

```
}
class MyCar : Cars  // derived class (child)
{
  public string cmodelName = "Mustang";  // Car field
}
class Program1
{
  static void Main(string[] args)
  {
    // Create a myCar object
    MyCar myCar = new MyCar();

    myCar.honk();
    Console.WriteLine(myCar.company + " " +
myCar.cmodelName);
  }
}
}
```

$mcs *.cs -out:main.exe
$mono main.exe
This is a brand new:
Ford Mustang

You can see that the parent class in the code is named as Cars while the child class in the code is named as MyCar. Inheritance is considered an important aspect of Object-oriented Programming (OOP). It is a particular mechanism in C# by which the child class is allowed to inherit different features of the parent class. The parent class, whose features are inherited by the child class is also known as the superclass or the base class. The child class which inherits the features of the parent class is dubbed as a subclass or derived class or extended class. The subclass also can add its own methods and fields besides inheriting methods and fields of the superclass.

The inheritance feature of C# classes tends to support the concept of reusability. When you intend to create a new class and there already exists one which includes some code that you want, you can derive a new class from an existing one. Take a look at another example of an inherited class.

```
using System;
namespace MyApp {

class Program1 {

    // data members
    public string cname;
    public string csubject;

    public void creaders(string cname, string csubject)
    {
        this.cname = cname;
        this.csubject = csubject;
        Console.WriteLine("My name is " + cname);
```

```csharp
        Console.WriteLine("My most favorite subject is as
follows: " + csubject);
    }
}

class Myclass : Program1 {

    // constructor of derived class
    public Myclass()
    {
        Console.WriteLine("This is the child class or inherited
class");
    }
}

// Driver class
class Sudo1 {

    // Main Method
    static void Main(string[] args)
    {

        // creating object of derived class
        Myclass g = new Myclass();

        g.creaders("Tom", "Physics");
    }
}
```

}

$mcs *.cs -out:main.exe

$mono main.exe

This is the child class or inherited class

My name is Tom

My most favorite subject is as follows: Physics

Polymorphism

The term polymorphism literally means "having multiple forms.". If you have read chemistry, you might have been acquainted with the term polymorphism. It occurs when many classes are generally related to each other by the method of inheritance. Inheritance allows programmers to inherit methods and fields from another class. Polymorphism makes use of the methods to perform many tasks. This will allow them to perform one action in several ways.

```
using System;
namespace MyApp
{
class Animalkingdom  // This is the Base class also known as
the parent class
{
  public void theanimalSound()
  {
    Console.WriteLine("Our animal is making a sound at the
moment");
  }
}
```

```csharp
class Cat : Animalkingdom  // This is the derived class (child)
{
  public void theanimalSound()
  {
    Console.WriteLine("The cat says: Meow Meow");
  }
}
class Horse : Animalkingdom  // This is the derived class
(child)
{
  public void theanimalSound()
  {
    Console.WriteLine("The horse says: Neigh Neigh");
  }
}
class Program1
{
  static void Main(string[] args)
  {
    Animalkingdom thisAnimal = new Animalkingdom();  //
Creating an Animal object
    Animalkingdom thisCat = new Cat();  // Creating a Pig
object
    Animalkingdom thisHorse = new Horse();  // Creating a
Dog object
    thisAnimal.theanimalSound();
    thisCat.theanimalSound();
    thisHorse.theanimalSound();
```

```
    }
  }
}
```

$mono main.exe

Our animal is making a sound at the moment

Our animal is making a sound at the moment

Our animal is making a sound at the moment

I am adding one more animal to the code.

```csharp
using System;
namespace MyApp
{
class Animalkingdom  // This is the Base class also known as
the parent class
{
  public void theanimalSound()
  {
    Console.WriteLine("Our animal is making a sound at the
moment");
  }
}
class Cat : Animalkingdom  // This is the derived class (child)
{
  public void theanimalSound()
  {
    Console.WriteLine("The cat says: Meow Meow");
  }
}
```

```csharp
class Horse : Animalkingdom  // This is the derived class
(child)
{
  public void theanimalSound()
  {
    Console.WriteLine("The horse says: Neigh Neigh");
  }
}
class Dog : Animalkingdom  // This is the derived class
(child)
{
  public void theanimalSound()
  {
    Console.WriteLine("The dog says: Bau Bau");
  }
}
class Program1
{
  static void Main(string[] args)
  {
    Animalkingdom thisAnimal = new Animalkingdom();  //
Creating an Animal object
    Animalkingdom thisCat = new Cat();  // Creating a Pig
object
    Animalkingdom thisHorse = new Horse();  // Creating a
Dog object
    Animalkingdom thisDog = new Dog();
```

```
      thisAnimal.theanimalSound();
      thisCat.theanimalSound();
      thisHorse.theanimalSound();
      thisDog.theanimalSound();
    }
  }
}
```

$mono main.exe

Our animal is making a sound at the moment

Our animal is making a sound at the moment

Our animal is making a sound at the moment

Our animal is making a sound at the moment

The output is not what you might be expecting. There is no mention of the type of sounds that the animals had been producing. The base class method has overridden the derived class method because they share the same name. You can add the virtual keyword to the method.

```
using System;
namespace MyApp
{
class Animalkingdom  // This is the Base class also known as
the parent class
{
  public virtual void theanimalSound()
  {
```

```csharp
      Console.WriteLine("Our animal is making a sound at the
moment");
  }
}
class Cat : Animalkingdom  // This is the derived class (child)
{
  public override void theanimalSound()
  {
    Console.WriteLine("The cat says: Meow Meow");
  }
}
class Horse : Animalkingdom  // This is the derived class
(child)
{
  public override void theanimalSound()
  {
    Console.WriteLine("The horse says: Neigh Neigh");
  }
}
class Dog : Animalkingdom  // This is the derived class
(child)
{
  public override void theanimalSound()
  {
    Console.WriteLine("The dog says: Bau Bau");
  }
}
class Program1
```

```
{
    static void Main(string[] args)
    {
    Animalkingdom thisAnimal = new Animalkingdom();  //
Creating an Animal object
    Animalkingdom thisCat = new Cat();  // Creating a Pig
object
    Animalkingdom thisHorse = new Horse();  // Creating a
Dog object
    Animalkingdom thisDog = new Dog();

    thisAnimal.theanimalSound();
    thisCat.theanimalSound();
    thisHorse.theanimalSound();
    thisDog.theanimalSound();
    }
}
}
```

$mcs *.cs -out:main.exe

$mono main.exe

Our animal is making a sound at the moment

The cat says: Meow Meow

The horse says: Neigh Neigh

The dog says: Bau Bau

Abstraction

Data abstraction is known as the process of hiding specific details and also showing the essential information to the user. You can achieve abstraction with interfaces or abstract classes. You can use the abstract keyword for methods and classes. An abstract class is a kind of restricted class that cannot be used for the creation of an object. The abstract method can be used in the abstract class. It lacks a body.

```
using System;
namespace MyApp
{
abstract class Animalkingdom  // This is the Base class also
known as the parent class
{
  public abstract void theanimalSound();
  public void csleep()
  {
    Console.WriteLine("Zzz");
  }
}
class Cat : Animalkingdom  // This is the derived class (child)
{
  public override void theanimalSound()
  {
    Console.WriteLine("The cat says: Meow Meow");
  }
}
class Horse : Animalkingdom  // This is the derived class
(child)
{
```

```csharp
  public override void theanimalSound()
  {
    Console.WriteLine("The horse says: Neigh Neigh");
  }
}
class Dog : Animalkingdom  // This is the derived class (child)
{
  public override void theanimalSound()
  {
    Console.WriteLine("The dog says: Bau Bau");
  }
}
class Program1
{
  static void Main(string[] args)
  {

    Animalkingdom thisCat = new Cat();  // Creating a Pig object
    thisCat.theanimalSound();
    thisCat.csleep();

    Animalkingdom thisHorse = new Horse();  // Creating a Dog object
    thisHorse.theanimalSound();
    thisHorse.csleep();
```

```
    Animalkingdom thisDog = new Dog();
    thisDog.theanimalSound();
    thisDog.csleep();
  }
 }
 }
```

$mcs *.cs -out:main.exe

$mono main.exe

The cat says: Meow Meow

Zzz

The horse says: Neigh Neigh

Zzz

The dog says: Bau Bau

Zzz

Interfaces

This is yet another method to achieve abstraction. Note the changes in the code.

```
using System;
namespace MyApp
{
interface IAnimalkingdom  // This is the Base class also
known as the parent class
{
  void theanimalSound();
}
```

```csharp
class Cat : IAnimalkingdom  // This is the derived class
(child)
{
  public void theanimalSound()
  {
    Console.WriteLine("The cat says: Meow Meow");
  }
}
class Horse : IAnimalkingdom  // This is the derived class
(child)
{
  public void theanimalSound()
  {
    Console.WriteLine("The horse says: Neigh Neigh");
  }
}
class Dog : IAnimalkingdom  // This is the derived class
(child)
{
  public void theanimalSound()
  {
    Console.WriteLine("The dog says: Bau Bau");
  }
}
class Program1
{
  static void Main(string[] args)
  {
```

```
    IAnimalkingdom thisCat = new Cat();  // Creating a Pig
object
    thisCat.theanimalSound();
    IAnimalkingdom thisHorse = new Horse();  // Creating a
Dog object
    thisHorse.theanimalSound();

    IAnimalkingdom thisDog = new Dog();
    thisDog.theanimalSound();
  }
}
}
$mcs *.cs -out:main.exe
$mono main.exe
The cat says: Meow Meow
The horse says: Neigh Neigh
The dog says: Bau Bau
```

Error Messages

Classes are complex and lengthy which raises the stakes of committing blunders. If you miss a curly brace or add an extra to the code, your program will return an error. As C# is a compiled language, it gets pretty much tough to spot the error. Therefore you need to write it cleanly so that if an error pops up, you can detect it and correct it. See the following error.

```
using System;
```

```
namespace MyApp
{
class Animalkingdom  // This is the Base class also known as
the parent class
{
  public void theanimalSound()
  {
    Console.WriteLine("Our animal is making a sound at the
moment");
  }
}
class Cat : Animalkingdom  // This is the derived class (child)
{
  public void theanimalSound()
  {
    Console.WriteLine("The cat says: Meow Meow");
  }
}
class Horse : Animalkingdom  // This is the derived class
(child)
{
  public void theanimalSound()
  {
    Console.WriteLine("The horse says: Neigh Neigh");
  }
}
class Dog : Animalkingdom  // This is the derived class
(child)
```

```
{
  public void theanimalSound()
  {
    Console.WriteLine("The dog says: Bau Bau");
  }
}
class Program1
{
  static void Main(string[] args)
  {
    Animalkingdom thisAnimal = new Animalkingdom();  // Creating an Animal object
    Animalkingdom thisCat = new Cat();  // Creating a Pig object
    Animalkingdom thisHorse = new Horse();  // Creating a Dog object
    Animakingdom thisDog = new Dog();

    thisAnimal.theanimalSound();
    thisCat.theanimalSound();
    thisHorse.theanimalSound();
    thisDog.theanimalSound();
  }
}
}
```

$mcs *.cs -out:main.exe

Compilation failed: 2 error(s), 3 warnings

main.cs(15,15): warning CS0108:
`MyApp.Cat.theanimalSound()' hides inherited member
`MyApp.Animalkingdom.theanimalSound()'. Use the new
keyword if hiding was intended
main.cs(7,15): (Location of the symbol related to previous
warning)
main.cs(23,15): warning CS0108:
`MyApp.Horse.theanimalSound()' hides inherited member
`MyApp.Animalkingdom.theanimalSound()'. Use the new
keyword if hiding was intended
main.cs(7,15): (Location of the symbol related to previous
warning)
main.cs(31,15): warning CS0108:
`MyApp.Dog.theanimalSound()' hides inherited member
`MyApp.Animalkingdom.theanimalSound()'. Use the new
keyword if hiding was intended
main.cs(7,15): (Location of the symbol related to previous
warning)
main.cs(44,5): error CS0246: The type or namespace name
`Animakingdom' could not be found. Are you missing an
assembly reference?
main.cs(49,5): error CS0841: A local variable `thisDog'
cannot be used before it is declared

I couldn't add a single l to the word animal and the entire program
is ruined with no hint of the error. You have to scan the entire code
and spot the error. See another misspelling error in the following
example.

```csharp
using System;
namespace MyApp
{
class Animalkingdom  // This is the Base class also known as
the parent class
{
  public void theanimalSound()
  {
    Console.WriteLine("Our animal is making a sound at the
moment");
  }
}
class Cat : Animalkingdom  // This is the derived class (child)
{
  public void theanimalSound()
  {
    Console.WriteLine("The cat says: Meow Meow");
  }
}
class Horse : Animalkingdom  // This is the derived class
(child)
{
  public void theanimalSound()
  {
    Console.riteLine("The horse says: Neigh Neigh");
  }
}
```

```csharp
class Dog : Animalkingdom  // This is the derived class
(child)
{
  public void theanimalSound()
  {
    Console.WriteLine("The dog says: Bau Bau");
  }
}
class Program1
{
  static void Main(string[] args)
  {
    Animalkingdom thisAnimal = new Animalkingdom();  //
Creating an Animal object
    Animalkingdom thisCat = new Cat();  // Creating a Pig
object
    Animalkingdom thisHorse = new Horse();  // Creating a
Dog object
    Animalkingdom thisDog = new Dog();

    thisAnimal.theanimalSound();
    thisCat.theanimalSound();
    thisHorse.theanimalSound();
    thisDog.theanimalSound();
  }
}
}
$mcs *.cs -out:main.exe
```

Compilation failed: 1 error(s), 3 warnings

main.cs(15,15): warning CS0108:

`MyApp.Cat.theanimalSound()' hides inherited member
`MyApp.Animalkingdom.theanimalSound()'. Use the new
keyword if hiding was intended

main.cs(7,15): (Location of the symbol related to previous
warning)

main.cs(23,15): warning CS0108:

`MyApp.Horse.theanimalSound()' hides inherited member
`MyApp.Animalkingdom.theanimalSound()'. Use the new
keyword if hiding was intended

main.cs(7,15): (Location of the symbol related to previous
warning)

main.cs(31,15): warning CS0108:

`MyApp.Dog.theanimalSound()' hides inherited member
`MyApp.Animalkingdom.theanimalSound()'. Use the new`
keyword if hiding was intended

main.cs(7,15): (Location of the symbol related to previous
warning)

main.cs(25,13): error CS0117: `System.Console' does not
contain a definition for `riteLine'

/usr/lib/mono/4.5/mscorlib.dll (Location of the symbol related
to previous error)

In the above error, I skipped a w in WriteLine. Can you understand
the error message? Not at the first look. But you can do that if you
read the message twice or thrice. See what happens if the names
you used as variables don't match. This one is more self-evident

than the previous errors. You may find it easier to detect them. However, you should read the error message and trying to decipher its meaning. In this way, if something similar pops up on your screen during programming, you will find it easier and quicker to fix. I will change the names of variables so they don't match.

```
using System;
namespace MyApp
{
class Animalkingdom  // This is the Base class also known as
the parent class
{
  public void theanimalSound()
  {
    Console.WriteLine("Our animal is making a sound at the
moment");
  }
}
class Cat : Animalkingdom  // This is the derived class (child)
{
  public void theanimalSound()
  {
    Console.WriteLine("The cat says: Meow Meow");
  }
}
class Horse : Animalkingdom  // This is the derived class
(child)
{
```

```csharp
    public void theanimalSound()
    {
      Console.WriteLine("The horse says: Neigh Neigh");
    }
}
class Dog : Animalkingdom  // This is the derived class
(child)
{
  public void theanimalSound()
  {
    Console.WriteLine("The dog says: Bau Bau");
  }
}
class Program1
{
  static void Main(string[] args)
  {
    Animalkingdom thisAnimal = new Animalkingdom();  //
Creating an Animal object
    Animalkingdom thisCat = new Cat();  // Creating a Pig
object
    Animalkingdom thisHorse = new Horse();  // Creating a
Dog object
    Animalkingdom thisDog = new Dog();

    thisAnimal.theanimalSound();
    MyCat.theanimalSound();
    MyHorse.theanimalSound();
```

```
    MyDog.theanimalSound();
  }
 }
}
```

$mcs *.cs -out:main.exe

Compilation failed: 3 error(s), 3 warnings

main.cs(15,15): warning CS0108:

`MyApp.Cat.theanimalSound()' hides inherited member
`MyApp.Animalkingdom.theanimalSound()'. Use the new
keyword if hiding was intended

main.cs(7,15): (Location of the symbol related to previous
warning)

main.cs(23,15): warning CS0108:

`MyApp.Horse.theanimalSound()' hides inherited member
`MyApp.Animalkingdom.theanimalSound()'. Use the new
keyword if hiding was intended

main.cs(7,15): (Location of the symbol related to previous
warning)

main.cs(31,15): warning CS0108:

`MyApp.Dog.theanimalSound()' hides inherited member
`MyApp.Animalkingdom.theanimalSound()'. Use the new
keyword if hiding was intended

main.cs(7,15): (Location of the symbol related to previous
warning)

main.cs(47,5): error CS0103: The name `MyCat' does not
exist in the current context

main.cs(48,5): error CS0103: The name `MyHorse' does not
exist in the current context

main.cs(49,5): error CS0103: The name `MyDog' does not exist in the current context

A common error that you may confront while you are creating a program is caused by missing any curly braces. See the following code.

```
using System;
namespace MyApp
{
class Animalkingdom  // This is the Base class also known as the parent class
{
  public void theanimalSound()
   {
     Console.WriteLine("Our animal is making a sound at the moment");
   }
}
class Cat : Animalkingdom  // This is the derived class (child)
{
  public void theanimalSound()
   {
     Console.WriteLine("The cat says: Meow Meow");
   }
}
class Horse : Animalkingdom  // This is the derived class (child)
```

```csharp
{
  public void theanimalSound()
  {
    Console.WriteLine("The horse says: Neigh Neigh");
  }
}
class Dog : Animalkingdom  // This is the derived class
(child)
{
  public void theanimalSound()
  {
    Console.WriteLine("The dog says: Bau Bau");
  }
}
class Program1
{
  static void Main(string[] args)
  {
    Animalkingdom thisAnimal = new Animalkingdom();  //
Creating an Animal object
    Animalkingdom thisCat = new Cat();  // Creating a Pig
object
    Animalkingdom thisHorse = new Horse();  // Creating a
Dog object
    Animalkingdom thisDog = new Dog();

    thisAnimal.theanimalSound();
    thisCat.theanimalSound();
```

```
    thisHorse.theanimalSound();
    thisDog.theanimalSound();
```

$mcs *.cs -out:main.exe

Compilation failed: 1 error(s), 0 warnings

main.cs(51,246): error CS1525: Unexpected symbol `end-of-file'

This error message clearly tells you that there is an unexpected symbol at the end of the file. Now see the following error.

```
using System;
namespace MyApp
{
class Animalkingdom  // This is the Base class also known as the parent class
{
  public void theanimalSound()
   {
    Console.WriteLine("Our animal is making a sound at the moment");
   }
}
class Cat : Animalkingdom  // This is the derived class (child)
{
  public void theanimalSound()
   {
    Console.WriteLine("The cat says: Meow Meow");
```

```csharp
class Horse : Animalkingdom  // This is the derived class
(child)
{
  public void theanimalSound()
  {
    Console.WriteLine("The horse says: Neigh Neigh");
  }
}
class Dog : Animalkingdom  // This is the derived class
(child)
{
  public void theanimalSound()
  {
    Console.WriteLine("The dog says: Bau Bau");
  }
}
class Program1
{
  static void Main(string[] args)
  {
    Animalkingdom thisAnimal = new Animalkingdom();  //
Creating an Animal object
    Animalkingdom thisCat = new Cat();  // Creating a Pig
object
    Animalkingdom thisHorse = new Horse();  // Creating a
Dog object
    Animalkingdom thisDog = new Dog();
```

thisAnimal.theanimalSound();
thisCat.theanimalSound();
thisHorse.theanimalSound();
thisDog.theanimalSound();

```
    }
}
}
```

$mcs *.cs -out:main.exe

Compilation failed: 6 error(s), 0 warnings

main.cs(20,0): error CS1525: Unexpected symbol `class'

main.cs(21,0): error CS1525: Unexpected symbol `{'

main.cs(22,2): error CS1525: Unexpected symbol `public'

main.cs(22,10): error CS1547: Keyword `void' cannot be used in this context

main.cs(22,28): error CS1525: Unexpected symbol `('

main.cs(52,246): error CS1525: Unexpected symbol `end-of-file'

This one is a bit confusing because everything is alright at the end of the file. However, there are a couple of wrong symbols in the file. You need to spot them and fill the vacant spot with the correct symbols. See the following error and spot what is missing in the program.

namespace MyApp
{

```csharp
class Animalkingdom  // This is the Base class also known as
the parent class
{
  public void theanimalSound()
   {
    Console.WriteLine("Our animal is making a sound at the
moment");
   }
}
class Cat : Animalkingdom  // This is the derived class (child)
{
  public void theanimalSound()
   {
    Console.WriteLine("The cat says: Meow Meow");
   }
}
class Horse : Animalkingdom  // This is the derived class
(child)
{
  public void theanimalSound()
   {
    Console.WriteLine("The horse says: Neigh Neigh");
   }
}
class Dog : Animalkingdom  // This is the derived class
(child)
{
  public void theanimalSound()
```

```
    {
      Console.WriteLine("The dog says: Bau Bau");
    }
}
class Program1
{
  static void Main(string[] args)
  {
    Animalkingdom thisAnimal = new Animalkingdom();  // Creating an Animal object
    Animalkingdom thisCat = new Cat();  // Creating a Pig object
    Animalkingdom thisHorse = new Horse();  // Creating a Dog object
    Animalkingdom thisDog = new Dog();

    thisAnimal.theanimalSound();
    thisCat.theanimalSound();
    thisHorse.theanimalSound();
    thisDog.theanimalSound();
  }
}
}
```

$mcs *.cs -out:main.exe

Compilation failed: 4 error(s), 3 warnings

main.cs(15,15): warning CS0108:

`MyApp.Cat.theanimalSound()' hides inherited member

`MyApp.Animalkingdom.theanimalSound()'. Use the new keyword if hiding was intended

main.cs(7,15): (Location of the symbol related to previous warning)

main.cs(23,15): warning CS0108:

`MyApp.Horse.theanimalSound()' hides inherited member `MyApp.Animalkingdom.theanimalSound()'. Use the new keyword if hiding was intended

main.cs(7,15): (Location of the symbol related to previous warning)

main.cs(31,15): warning CS0108:

`MyApp.Dog.theanimalSound()' hides inherited member `MyApp.Animalkingdom.theanimalSound()'. Use the new keyword if hiding was intended

main.cs(7,15): (Location of the symbol related to previous warning)

main.cs(9,5): error CS0103: The name `Console' does not exist in the current context

main.cs(17,5): error CS0103: The name `Console' does not exist in the current context

main.cs(25,5): error CS0103: The name `Console' does not exist in the current context

main.cs(33,5): error CS0103: The name `Console' does not exist in the current context

A hint is that something is missing at the top of the file. This happens more often when you are copying code from one file to another. If you see the error on the screen that the compiler has found an unexpected symbol in the program, you should know that you might have missed a semicolon or a curly brace. The following error message does tell you that a semicolon is either missing or is in excess, but it doesn't tell where the error lies. Just like other errors, you have to find it yourself. Take a look and try to find the error.

```
using System
namespace MyApp
{
class Animalkingdom;  // This is the Base class also known as the parent class
{
  public void theanimalSound()
  {
    Console.WriteLine("Our animal is making a sound at the moment");
  }
}
class Cat : Animalkingdom  // This is the derived class (child)
{
  public void theanimalSound()
  {
    Console.WriteLine("The cat says: Meow Meow");
  }
}
class Horse : Animalkingdom  // This is the derived class (child)
```

```csharp
{
  public void theanimalSound()
  {
    Console.WriteLine("The horse says: Neigh Neigh");
  }
}
class Dog : Animalkingdom  // This is the derived class
(child)
{
  public void theanimalSound()
  {
    Console.WriteLine("The dog says: Bau Bau");
  }
}
class Program1
{
  static void Main(string[] args)
  {
    Animalkingdom thisAnimal = new Animalkingdom();  //
Creating an Animal object
    Animalkingdom thisCat = new Cat();  // Creating a Pig
object
    Animalkingdom thisHorse = new Horse();  // Creating a
Dog object
    Animalkingdom thisDog = new Dog();

    thisAnimal.theanimalSound();
    thisCat.theanimalSound();
```

```
    thisHorse.theanimalSound();
    thisDog.theanimalSound();
  }
}
}
```

$mcs *.cs -out:main.exe

Compilation failed: 7 error(s), 0 warnings

main.cs(3,0): error CS1525: Unexpected symbol `namespace',
expecting `.', `::', `;', `<', or `='

main.cs(5,19): error CS1525: Unexpected symbol `;',
expecting `(', `:', `{', or `where'

main.cs(7,9): error CS1525: Unexpected symbol `void',
expecting `(', `:', `{', or `where'

main.cs(9,4): error CS1525: Unexpected symbol `Console',
expecting `(', `:', `{', or `where'

main.cs(9,21): error CS1525: Unexpected symbol `(',
expecting `(', `:', `{', or `where'

main.cs(10,3): error CS1514: Unexpected symbol `}',
expecting `.' or `{'

main.cs(52,0): error CS1525: Unexpected symbol `}'

So I added an extra semicolon to the program; the compiler returned this in the form of an error. Now in the next example, I will remove a couple of semicolons. See the error message and try to familiarize yourself with this error message so that you may fix this kind of problem head-on while you are writing a program.

    using System

```
namespace MyApp
{
class Animalkingdom  // This is the Base class also known as
the parent class
{
  public void theanimalSound()
  {
    Console.WriteLine("Our animal is making a sound at the
moment")
  }
}
class Cat : Animalkingdom  // This is the derived class (child)
{
  public void theanimalSound()
  {
    Console.WriteLine("The cat says: Meow Meow")
  }
}
class Horse : Animalkingdom  // This is the derived class
(child)
{
  public void theanimalSound()
  {
    Console.WriteLine("The horse says: Neigh Neigh")
  }
}
class Dog : Animalkingdom  // This is the derived class
(child)
```

```csharp
{
  public void theanimalSound()
  {
    Console.WriteLine("The dog says: Bau Bau");
  }
}
class Program1
{
  static void Main(string[] args)
  {
    Animalkingdom thisAnimal = new Animalkingdom();  // Creating an Animal object
    Animalkingdom thisCat = new Cat();  // Creating a Pig object
    Animalkingdom thisHorse = new Horse();  // Creating a Dog object
    Animalkingdom thisDog = new Dog();

    thisAnimal.theanimalSound();
    thisCat.theanimalSound();
    thisHorse.theanimalSound();
    thisDog.theanimalSound();
  }
}
}
```

$mcs *.cs -out:main.exe

Compilation failed: 4 error(s), 0 warnings

main.cs(3,0): error CS1525: Unexpected symbol `namespace',
expecting `.', `::', `;', `<', or `='
main.cs(10,3): error CS1002: ; expected
main.cs(18,3): error CS1002: ; expected
main.cs(26,3): error CS1002: ; expected

Another common mistake that programmers make is that they miss out on writing the right upper case and lower case letters. In the following error message, I will deliberately miss out on using capital letters where I must use them. See the error message and familiarize yourself with it to fix it if the same pops up while you are writing a program. See the following example.

```
using System;
namespace MyApp
{
class Animalkingdom  // This is the Base class also known as the parent class
{
  public void theanimalSound()
  {
    Console.WriteLine("Our animal is making a sound at the moment");
  }
}
class Cat : Animalkingdom  // This is the derived class (child)
{
  public void theanimalSound()
```

```
    {
      Console.WriteLine("The cat says: Meow Meow");
    }
  }
class Horse : Animalkingdom  // This is the derived class
(child)
  {
    public void theanimalSound()
    {
      Console.WriteLine("The horse says: Neigh Neigh");
    }
  }
class Dog : Animalkingdom  // This is the derived class
(child)
  {
    public void theanimalSound()
    {
      Console.WriteLine("The dog says: Bau Bau");
    }
  }
class Program1
  {
    static void Main(string[] args)
    {
      Animalkingdom thisAnimal = new Animalkingdom();  //
Creating an Animal object
      Animalkingdom thisCat = new cat();  // Creating a Pig
object
```

Animalkingdom thisHorse = new horse(); // Creating a Dog object

Animalkingdom thisDog = new dog();

thisAnimal.theanimalSound();
thisCat.theanimalSound();
thisHorse.theanimalSound();
thisDog.theanimalSound();
  }
}
}

$mcs *.cs -out:main.exe

Compilation failed: 3 error(s), 3 warnings

main.cs(15,15): warning CS0108:

`MyApp.Cat.theanimalSound()' hides inherited member `MyApp.Animalkingdom.theanimalSound()'. Use the new keyword if hiding was intended

main.cs(7,15): (Location of the symbol related to previous warning)

main.cs(23,15): warning CS0108:

`MyApp.Horse.theanimalSound()' hides inherited member `MyApp.Animalkingdom.theanimalSound()'. Use the new keyword if hiding was intended

main.cs(7,15): (Location of the symbol related to previous warning)

main.cs(31,15): warning CS0108:

`MyApp.Dog.theanimalSound()' hides inherited member

`MyApp.Animalkingdom.theanimalSound()'. Use the new keyword if hiding was intended
main.cs(7,15): (Location of the symbol related to previous warning)
main.cs(42,33): error CS0246: The type or namespace name `cat' could not be found. Are you missing an assembly reference?
main.cs(43,35): error CS0246: The type or namespace name `horse' could not be found. Are you missing an assembly reference?
main.cs(44,33): error CS0246: The type or namespace name `dog' could not be found. Are you missing an assembly reference?

The next error is a simple one; that's why you should decipher the error message yourself and try to spot it.

```
using System;
namespace MyApp
{
class Animalkingdom  // This is the Base class also known as the parent class
{
  public void theanimalSound
  {
    Console.WriteLine("Our animal is making a sound at the moment");
  }
```

```csharp
}
class Cat : Animalkingdom  // This is the derived class (child)
{
  public void theanimalSound
  {
    Console.WriteLine("The cat says: Meow Meow");
  }
}
class Horse : Animalkingdom  // This is the derived class
(child)
{
  public void theanimalSound
  {
    Console.WriteLine("The horse says: Neigh Neigh");
  }
}
class Dog : Animalkingdom  // This is the derived class
(child)
{
  public void theanimalSound
  {
    Console.WriteLine("The dog says: Bau Bau");
  }
}
class Program1
{
  static void Main(string[] args)
  {
```

```
        Animalkingdom thisAnimal = new Animalkingdom();  //
Creating an Animal object
        Animalkingdom thisCat = new Cat;  // Creating a Pig object
        Animalkingdom thisHorse = new Horse;  // Creating a Dog
object
        Animalkingdom thisDog = new Dog;

        thisAnimal.theanimalSound;
        thisCat.theanimalSound;
        thisHorse.theanimalSound;
        thisDog.theanimalSound;
    }
}
}
```

$mcs *.cs -out:main.exe

Compilation failed: 11 error(s), 0 warnings

main.cs(7,10): error CS0547:

`MyApp.Animalkingdom.theanimalSound': property or
indexer cannot have void type

main.cs(9,5): error CS1014: A get or set accessor expected

main.cs(15,10): error CS0547: `MyApp.Cat.theanimalSound':
property or indexer cannot have void type

main.cs(17,5): error CS1014: A get or set accessor expected

main.cs(23,10): error CS0547:

`MyApp.Horse.theanimalSound': property or indexer cannot
have void type

main.cs(25,5): error CS1014: A get or set accessor expected

main.cs(31,10): error CS0547:

`MyApp.Dog.theanimalSound': property or indexer cannot have void type

main.cs(33,5): error CS1014: A get or set accessor expected

main.cs(42,35): error CS1525: Unexpected symbol `;', expecting `(', `[', or `{'

main.cs(43,39): error CS1525: Unexpected symbol `;', expecting `(', `[', or `{'

main.cs(44,35): error CS1525: Unexpected symbol `;', expecting `(', `[', or `{'

I will explain in this error the absence of the inverted commas. Sometimes they are too much that you lose track of them while writing a program. See the following error message and try to understand it so that you may fix it in the future.

```
using System;
namespace MyApp
{
class Animalkingdom  // This is the Base class also known as the parent class
{
  public void theanimalSound()
  {
    Console.WriteLine("Our animal is making a sound at the moment);
  }
}
```

```
class Cat : Animalkingdom  // This is the derived class (child)
{
  public void theanimalSound()
  {
    Console.WriteLine("The cat says: Meow Meow');
  }
}
class Horse : Animalkingdom  // This is the derived class
(child)
{
  public void theanimalSound()
  {
    Console.WriteLine("The horse says: Neigh Neigh);
  }
}
class Dog : Animalkingdom  // This is the derived class
(child)
{
  public void theanimalSound()
  {
    Console.WriteLine("The dog says: Bau Bau);
  }
}
class Program1
{
  static void Main(string[] args)
  {
```

Animalkingdom thisAnimal = new Animalkingdom(); // Creating an Animal object

Animalkingdom thisCat = new Cat(); // Creating a Pig object

Animalkingdom thisHorse = new Horse(); // Creating a Dog object

Animalkingdom thisDog = new Dog();

thisAnimal.theanimalSound();
thisCat.theanimalSound();
thisHorse.theanimalSound();
thisDog.theanimalSound();
}
}
}

$mcs *.cs -out:main.exe

Compilation failed: 12 error(s), 0 warnings

main.cs(9,67): error CS1010: Newline in constant

main.cs(10,2): error CS1525: Unexpected symbol `}', expecting `)' or `,'

main.cs(10,3): error CS1002: ; expected

main.cs(17,49): error CS1010: Newline in constant

main.cs(18,2): error CS1525: Unexpected symbol `}', expecting `)' or `,'

main.cs(18,3): error CS1002: ; expected

main.cs(25,52): error CS1010: Newline in constant

main.cs(26,2): error CS1525: Unexpected symbol `}', expecting `)' or `,' main.cs(26,3): error CS1002: ; expected

main.cs(33,46): error CS1010: Newline in constant

main.cs(34,2): error CS1525: Unexpected symbol `}',
expecting `)' or `,'

main.cs(34,3): error CS1002: ; expected

In the following error code, I will use the switch statement to see which kind of errors you may experience. I will change the case of keywords like a switch in the program. See the following example.

```
using System.IO;
using System;
class Program
{
    static void Main()
    {
      Int day = 1;
Switch (day)
{
  Case 1:
    Console.WriteLine("We will start construction of the office on Monday");
    break;
  Case 2:
    Console.WriteLine("We will start construction of the office on Tuesday");
    break;
  Case 3:
```

```
    Console.WriteLine("We will start construction of the office
on Wednesday");
    break;
 case 4:
    Console.WriteLine("We will start construction of the office
on Thursday");
    break;
 case 5:
    Console.WriteLine("We will start construction of the office
on Friday");
    break;
 case 6:
    Console.WriteLine("We will start construction of the office
on Saturday");
    break;
 case 7:
    Console.WriteLine("We will start construction of the office
on Sunday");
    break;
}
   }
}
```

$mcs *.cs -out:main.exe

Compilation failed: 15 error(s), 0 warnings

main.cs(10,0): error CS1525: Unexpected symbol `{'

main.cs(11,7): error CS1525: Unexpected symbol `1'

main.cs(11,8): error CS1525: Unexpected symbol `:'

main.cs(14,7): error CS1525: Unexpected symbol `2'

main.cs(14,8): error CS1525: Unexpected symbol `:'

main.cs(17,7): error CS1525: Unexpected symbol `3'

main.cs(17,8): error CS1525: Unexpected symbol `:'

main.cs(20,2): error CS1525: Unexpected symbol `case'

main.cs(20,8): error CS1525: Unexpected symbol `:'

main.cs(23,2): error CS1525: Unexpected symbol `case'

main.cs(23,8): error CS1525: Unexpected symbol `:'

main.cs(26,2): error CS1525: Unexpected symbol `case'

main.cs(26,8): error CS1525: Unexpected symbol `:'

main.cs(29,2): error CS1525: Unexpected symbol `case'

main.cs(29,8): error CS1525: Unexpected symbol `:'

In the following code sample, you will see what happens if you misspell the keywords in a program.

```
using System.IO;
using System;
class Program1
{
   stati vid Main()
   {
     int day = 1;
switch (day)
{
  case 1:
    Consle.WriteLine("We will start construction of the office
on Monday");
    break;
```

```
case 2:
    Consle.WriteLine("We will start construction of the office
on Tuesday");
    break;
case 3:
    Consle.WriteLine("We will start construction of the office
on Wednesday");
    break;
case 4:
    Consle.WriteLine("We will start construction of the office
on Thursday");
    break;
case 5:
    Console.WriteLine("We will start construction of the office
on Friday");
    break;
case 6:
    Console.WriteLine("We will start construction of the office
on Saturday");
    break;
case 7:
    Console.WriteLine("We will start construction of the office
on Sunday");
    break;
}
    }
}
$mcs *.cs -out:main.exe
```

Compilation failed: 2 error(s), 0 warnings

main.cs(6,18): error CS1519: Unexpected symbol `Main' in class, struct, or interface member declaration

main.cs(6,15): error CS1520: Class, struct, or interface method must have a return type

In the next example, you will see what error message is likely to be displayed if you miss out on a symbol in a while loop.

```
using System.IO;
using System;
class Program1
{
    static void Main()
    {
        int x = 0 // this is the initialization
while (x < 50) // here is the condition
{
    Console.WriteLine("x = {0}", x);
    x++; // this is the increment
    }
    }
}
```

$mcs *.cs -out:main.exe

Compilation failed: 4 error(s), 0 warnings

main.cs(10,0): error CS1525: Unexpected symbol `while'

main.cs(12,34): error CS0128: A local variable named `x' is already defined in this scope main.cs(12,34): error CS1525: Unexpected symbol `)'

main.cs(17,0): error CS1525: Unexpected symbol `}'

A semicolon was missing in the above code sample. In the next example, I will remove () from the while loop and see what results I receive.

```
using System.IO;
using System;
class Program1
{
    static void Main
    {
        int x = 0; // this is the initialization
while (x < 50) // here is the condition
{
    Console.WriteLine("x = {0}", x);
    x++; // this is the increment
    }
    }
}
```

$mcs *.cs -out:main.exe

Compilation failed: 3 error(s), 0 warnings

main.cs(6,12): error CS0547: `Program1.Main': property or indexer cannot have void type

main.cs(8,8): error CS1014: A get or set accessor expected

main.cs(17,0): error CS1525: Unexpected symbol `}'

Chapter Nine

Writing Secure Code

Programming is generally described as the process which leads a computing problem from the original formulation to the executable program. The process generally involves different activities such as analysis, developing understanding, generation of algorithms, and verification of the essential algorithms including accuracy and the utilization of resources. It also includes the coding of different algorithms in a particular programming language.

Many C# developers don't write unit test methods for different non-public assemblies. C# enables you to boost visibility in between assembly internals and other different assemblies. Security is considered a big topic when it comes to coding and programming. When you have an application in C#, the first thing you need to do is secure from application from being attacked by malicious hackers or from being used for things it was not meant to be used for. At the start of the electronic age, security is normally performed by the method of obfuscation. If you have built an application and you want it to stay secure, you can hide it and no one will ever know where to find it. It would remain secure.

Security is and ought to be considered an integral part of every system you write. It is possible that your application may not contain any sensitive data, but will be used to get other information that is saved on your machine? Attackers might use it to gain access to a network that you have deemed forbidden.

The two major parts of security are known as authentication and authorization. Authentication is defined as the process of making sure that a user has the authentication to access the application. The most widely known method of authentication requires a username and a password. You also can use a thumbprint method for the purpose. Authentication suggests that you ensure that a user possesses the authority to do what he or she is requesting to do. File permissions are considered a good example of this. Some app developers don't let users delete system-only files.

However, there is more to security than merely usernames and passwords. This chapter will walk you through how to make your C# programs secure from outside attacks.

Secure Design

Security usually takes a good amount of work while you are designing software. If you break down the process into tiny chunks, you will find out that it would be a lot easier to accomplish. You have to take up a systematic approach to ensure the security of your systems. Different applications possess different artifacts that require protection, but all applications usually have something that needs to be secured. If there is a database in your application, it is the most important item for protection.

The server should be high-rated if you want better security. Even if you build a simple program that is a single-user application, you must not let any outsider to a user the application for breaking into the computer of the user.

Documentation

Describe what your application is. The description becomes a functional overview of the application. Describe how your application accomplishes the tasks at the highest level. If you take a look at a Software Architecture Overview diagram, you will know which services and machines have what job to do.

When you have created the document that describes the job of the software, you must break out different individual pieces of the software. If you have set up the software in the component fashion, the methods and classes show functional decomposition. The final result of this breaking down the software is taking a look at the individual pieces and decide which components must be protected.

When you have created a list of components that you ought to protect, you must tackle the tough part. You need to put two and two together. If your application tends to connect to a database, you must imagine that this connection needs to be intercepted by some third party.

Threat Model

You must create a threat model for which you have to categorize different potential threats to the software. The easiest way to remember different categories of threats is by using the STRIDE method.

Security is more often described as a negative property. You can label a system as secure if there is no danger of attack. To access the system's security, you need to look at and analyze all the possible threats that are posed against your system. The STRIDE model is considered a useful tool to help you classify these threats.

Microsoft develops it to classify potential threats on the server. Each alphabet in the word STRIDE represents a potential threat.

Spoofing

Most of the security systems tend to rely on the authentication and identification of the users. Spoofing attacks largely consist of using another user's credentials without his or her knowledge. Typical spoofing threats target weak authentication mechanisms. It targets those that have simple passwords like 4 digit password. Attackers access personal information quite easily such as the place of birth and the date of birth.

Tampering

Only authorized users are allowed to modify a system or the data it uses. If an attacker can tamper it, it results in some serious consequences on the usage of the system. If the attacker can add or remove a bunch of functional elements, for instance, some important data gets destroyed or modified.

Repudiation

Attackers need to hide malicious activity to avoid getting detected or blocked. They may try to repudiate the actions they have already performed such as erasing them from the logs or by spoofing different credentials of any other user.

Information Disclosure

Many systems keep confidential information. Attackers aim at securing and getting hold of that information. It also is known as data breaches.

Denial of Service

A system is deployed generally for a particular purpose whether it be a banking application or any kind of integrated media management that is installed on a vehicle. In some cases, attackers will show interest in the prevention of regular users for accessing the system. This can be for blackmailing a person or for extortion of money from the owner of a system. Ransomware is an example of such a threat.

Privilege

Once a system identifies a user, they have some kind of privilege which is that they are authorized for performing certain actions, but not all of the actions. An attacker might try to get additional privileges by spoofing a user with higher privileges or just by tampering the system and changing their respective privileges.

All these threats ought to be determined in a certain outline under the functions that would expose the threat. The strategy gives you a discrete list of threats and also focuses the security hardening on different parts of the application that would pose the greatest security risk.

You should rate the risk by defining what the potential for damage is. For example, you may calculate the dollar cost of the company for the breach. You ought to calculate how far a potential hacker can go in terms of exploiting our system. You also should calculate the number of users who have been affected. Try to find out who they are. The level of difficulty by which you can discover the threat also ought to be determined.

Common Mistakes

The most common mistake programmers make is using string concatenation technique in the wrong way. In other programming languages, concatenation can be done by inserting a plus sign between the strings. This is considered inefficient and fragile. C# offers StringBuilder method to perform the same task. The method is useful for complex operations. For example, you can deploy it if you have to concatenate one long list to another and display the output to the user or channelize the output to a database for storage purposes.

The second most common mistake that programmers make is that they don't log errors when they are writing the code. You have seen that I carefully documented different kinds of error messages that I received from the compiler, and presented them to you so that you can use them as a reference whenever you see the same, and fix them. If you develop the habit of documenting the error messages whenever the compiler throws one, you will be able to fix the errors in the code faster than before. Log your errors and the next you will see one, you will know its background.

The third mistake that can be easily avoided is using var despite knowing which data type is in use. When you use var, you allow the compiler to decide upon the datatype of the variable. The fact is that compiler may be wrong. It will not always detect the correct datatype. Better define the datatype yourself. Besides decreasing the chance of error, it will improve the readability of your code, which is better if a colleague in the office has to read your code for the purpose of its betterment.

Conclusion

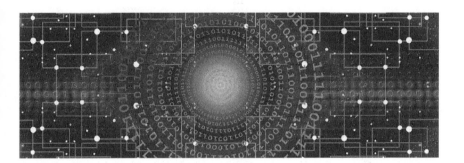

Now that you have made it to the end of the book, you should be able to practice the different features of C# programming. The key lies in practicing more by using different variables and methods. Experiment with the code and learn each step.

C# offers an immense variety of toolsets and different frameworks that you can use while programming. Microsoft generally backs all these frameworks and toolsets. Any developer will admit that Visual Studio is feature-rich and powerful development environments that exist in the market. The .NET framework offers hundreds of libraries for the building of websites, working with the file system and the implementation of security.

I hope that this book has equipped you with the right skills and techniques and that you will be able to program by using C#. You can keep this book as a pocketbook that you can use whenever you are writing or practicing a code. Take the sample codes as the right track to follow and gradually learn. I have tried to keep the context of the book as simple and easy-to-read as I could so that even a beginner may find in it the right material.

This book dealt with the most basic topics like strings, variables, data types, and other stuff like that. You learned about the basics of C# like strings, substrings, and different properties of strings. Strings and integers are the most common data types that you might have noticed on several occasions in the code. I have used both of them in almost all of my codes. You have learned about C# loops such as the while loop, do-while loop, for loop, and foreach loop. These topics are really interesting and can help you create programs that involve mathematical calculations. These types of elements are used in the programs that are created for cash counters. They will do the math for you in the blink of an eye. You have also learned about C# arrays and lists which are immensely helpful when you are creating a game in C#. You can allow the players to be more interactive while playing the game. You have also learned about the most important aspect of C# which is object-oriented programming (OOP). This chapter contained classes that are used to model real-life objects in the world of programming. I created a dog, a cat, and a car class for you to understand how you can create different objects and give them certain features so that they can fulfill your specific programming needs. I hope you have practiced this section quite well, and even if you have not, you should do that even if you have now completed the book. You must be an expert at OOP; that's why I have dedicated two chapters for this section. C# classes have different features and you must get yourself acquainted with them before you start writing your program.

References

http://www.scfilmvideo.com/download/temp/0470563486.For.Dummies.CSharp.2010.All-in-One.For.Dummies.Apr.2010.pdf

https://www.w3schools.com/cs/cs_arrays.asp

https://www.w3schools.com/cs/cs_for_loop.asp

https://www.w3schools.com/cs/cs_user_input.asp'

https://www.w3schools.com/cs/cs_conditions.asp

https://www.learncs.org/en/Lists#:~:text=Lists%20in%20C%23%20are%20very,called%20numbers%20which%20holds%20integers.

https://www.tutorialsteacher.com/csharp/csharp-list

https://www.w3schools.com/cs/cs_break.asp

https://www.w3schools.com/cs/cs_oop.asp

https://www.freelancer.com/community/articles/top-16-c-programming-tips-tricks

https://www.w3schools.com/cs/cs_classes.asp

https://www.w3schools.com/cs/cs_inheritance.asp

https://www.futurelearn.com/courses/cyber-security/0/steps/19631